Slaves to the Rhythm

A Love Story

by
Terry Connell

2

For my family with love...

...and plenty of paint!

3

The past is not dead. In fact, it's not even past.

William Faulkner

TABLE OF CONTENTS

Foreword

I finished the first edits of this book in the spring of 1994 and spent the next year trying to get it published. I sent sample chapters to at least a hundred different agents and publishers, believing they would be moved by what I had written; a firsthand account of taking care of my partner, Stephan, who died from AIDS complications in January, 1993. The feedback I got was an odd combination of support with a strong dash of fiscal realism.

Everyone liked my writing style. They said the story was "relevant" and "powerfully told." Not a bad note on the quality of the book and its subject matter. There was even an editor at Vanity Fair who offered to run a chapter of my book, if (and it was a big if), if, I could find a publisher. But this was the early nineties, and back then; AIDS was a scary dark shadow hanging over the gay community. Back then, no one talked about AIDS. The world took on what I would call a "less is more approach" – the less we know, the more we can claim ignorance.

With public awareness lacking and the gay community only starting to mobilize, my story was a little too real for a country in denial. Agents and publishers told me over and over there was no market for "my kind of book." But my efforts weren't fruitless. The Philadelphia Inquirer Sunday Magazine and Philadelphia Gay News each ran a chapter. It was a small victory, but one that allowed me to say I was a published writer.

After that, I put my manuscript away and focused on how to rebuild my life after losing Stephan. One thing was clear to me early on in my new role as AIDS widow, I needed to change it up in a big way. There were too many ghosts in Philadelphia, hiding around corners and looking at me from empty windows. More than once, a simple walk through town resulted in a crying jag for blocks; our favorite restaurant, the Jazz Dance Center, Bambi's Cleaners in South Philly were just a few triggers. I wasn't sure how or even where I was going, but I gave myself a year to figure it out. I had to leave this town or I was going to suffocate.

Through a random series of connections, I found my way to Boston, where I enrolled in the New England School of Acupuncture. My goal was to work at Boston's AIDS Care Project (ACP), one of the first holistic public health programs in the country. It was a rough few years in school trying to wrap my mind around this whole new way of looking at the body. But I found a few classmates that were my kind of crazy – and we struggled through anatomy and theory and point location together.

Four years after landing in Boston, I was a licensed acupuncturist and began working at AIDS Care Project. Without question, it the best job I ever had. I worked with the most dedicated, talented, passionate healers, and together, we developed treatment protocols that were changing how people with HIV/AIDS were living. Working at AIDS Care Project changed my life. Quite honestly, that clinic saved my life. It gave me, this broken, lost man, purpose – and sanctuary. I am so proud of the work we did there; it was a really special place.

After ten years, I left ACP and began working in a small private acupuncture practice of my own, adding yoga teacher to my bag of tricks. It's hard to describe to describe my life since leaving Philly, except to say that I continue to grow and learn... and think about Stephan a lot. I miss his easy ways, his point of view, his laugh... even his smell.

I try to imagine what Stephan would say about the life I've made for myself. Sometimes I hear his voice in my head while I'm with my friends or just hanging out in my apartment. He would be impressed with what I have accomplished in his absence... and would still roll his eyes at my bad housekeeping.

If there were one thing he'd be most pleased about, it is the way things have improved with my family. The tension I used to feel with every interaction has softened quite a bit. I still don't agree with the strict Catholic views many of my family hold onto. At the same time, I know they don't agree with how I live my life. Still, there's plenty of room in the middle. As the saying goes, time heals all wounds. Though to be honest, the scars can still be distracting, and painful, at times.

This book has traveled with me over the years, occasionally coming up in conversation or shared with certain people when they've asked. But in Spring, 2009, my "maybe someday" notion of publishing "Slaves" took on new urgency when I received a rough draft of our family tree in the mail, a project my father had been working on for years.

I have to say, given how well things had been feeling between me and my dad, I was surprised at how quickly – and strongly – those old feelings of anger and hurt surfaced looking through the pages he sent. I heard myself say, "It just doesn't fucking end!"

Truth be told, I never really expected to see Stephan's name included in our family tree, at least in not my Irish Catholic father's version of it. Still, it felt like my heart was ripped open when I read the section he had written about me. It was surreal, actually, to see how easily someone could erase a few facts in another's life and then present an incomplete picture as true. It is one of my biggest confusions in life, to watch over and over how a beautiful and heartfelt faith can be so cruel in its expression.

I felt stuck. How could I allow my father his faith and beliefs while still giving my life its complete expression? I didn't want to fight with my Dad; I wasn't interested in making him wrong. We'd grown past that. I knew how his beliefs sustained and nurtured him (and my mother). I didn't want to take that away from him.

At the same time, I knew I couldn't – I *wouldn't* – stay silent.

So here I am, returning to these pages written almost twenty years ago, though I am asking them to claim a different space. When I first wrote this book, my intention was to mark a certain place in time, to bear witness to the early years, when AIDS was a death sentence and a community stood helpless as its brothers and sisters succumbed.

But now? Now, my intention is quite simple: claim my rightful place in my family's history, honestly and completely.

Before going any further, I would like to offer a few comments on the design and editorial decisions I made in putting this book together, especially given my anger at my father's editorial efforts in our family tree.

First, a writer and acquaintance that read an early version of this book said that he wanted to know more about the "characters" of my story. He said, "Who are Terry and Stephan? How did they get to where they are when we meet them in your book?" To answer these questions, I have added chapters that follow my life from birth up to meeting Stephan at the age of twenty-eight. Every other chapter chronicles a different part of my life in a family that I loved – and feared.

Second, and in my mind, most important: None of what you are about to read would have been possible without the selfless, boundless love of Stephan's family and some close friends. I would often fill the pages of my journal describing the generosity and patience they offered. Wanting to honor them, I tried to include everyone in an early draft of this book. Unfortunately, when looking at the flow and logic of telling this story, there was a confusing energy to the names that would come and go, and paragraphs that didn't connect to anything, except that I knew the people in them. In order to keep the "story" of Stephan and me as simple as possible, I decided to edit my book with a focus primarily on our relationship.

This choice in no way reflects how I feel about those people who helped take care of Stephan – and me. It was the love and constant support of our friends and family that created what I can only describe as a sacred space, where the most profound moments in our relationship occurred.

In the following pages, there are quite a few times where I mention my writing. I did, in fact, complete one short story during my last year with Stephan. It is titled "The Tire Swing." I have a few other unfinished stories that never got past the first or second draft. They sit in my computer, hidden away in the same file as the rest of me half-written stories, waiting to see if I'll ever get back to finish them.

Finally, when an editor reviewed my manuscript, she suggested that AIDS "needed a voice and a context" in my story. I understood exactly what she meant. In the late '80s and early '90s, AIDS changed everything about our culture, from how we had sex, to fund-raising, to medical research. Even politics and religion felt the effects of the AIDS epidemic. AIDS silenced a generation of artists, leaders, and activists we will forever miss, but it also called forth the most unlikely of heroes.

To provide some context for the epidemic, I created a simple AIDS timeline to fit within the years of our story. This is by no means a definitive, but it helps illustrate what was happening in the early days of a health crisis that gripped a nation, and it shows how far we've come since. I used the following websites to collect the information presented: thebody.com, kff.org, aegis.com, about.com, and wikipedia.org.

In order to respect the privacy of some involved in the stories included here, I have changed the names of some people and places.

T.C.

November 9, 2010

AIDS Timeline #1

On <u>June 5, 1981</u>, in the Morbidity and Mortality Weekly Report the CDC reported that between October 1980-May 1981, 5 active homosexuals were treated for confirmed pneumocystis carinii pneumonia (PCP). All 5 patients showed severe immune deficiency and had confirmed previous or current cytomegalovirus and candida mucosal infection.

<u>July 1981</u>, The New York Times ran the article, "Rare Cancer seen in 41 Homosexuals."

By the <u>end of 1981</u>, 422 people have been diagnosed with AIDS, 159 have died from the disease.

<u>July 27, 1982</u>, the term AIDS, acquired immune deficiency syndrome, is used for the first time The first US Congressional Hearings on HIV/AIDS was held in 1982.

<u>By 1984</u>, PCP pneumonia (pneumocystis jrioveci carinii) was recognized as one of several infections often found in people with HIV/AIDS along with a rare cancer known as Karposi Sarcoma. The treatment for PCP was a drug called Pentamadine, administered either by IV injection or drip or through oral inhalation (nebulizer).

January 5

Just eight more days of treatment for pneumonia left (maybe seven, I'm not sure anymore). Yesterday was probably the worst since he was discharged. Stephan was tired and light-headed all day, and there's this constant metallic taste in his mouth. We've been keeping a steady supply of Italian water ice, and sorbet on hand; this seems to help keep his mouth cool and get rid of the taste. Every night, on the way home from work, I stop at "The Wizard of Ice" on South Street. Stephan likes the watermelon flavor the best.

Despite all the side effects, his spirits seem pretty positive. Last night he said, "This isn't my last hurrah. I'll be OK. When it's time for me to go, I'll know it." I'm doing my best to be supportive, but I don't feel so optimistic.

On the plus side, Donna, the nurse who comes to work with Stephan, is friendly, sensitive, and very efficient. I leave them alone now and either write a little or take a walk. Stephan says she's never met a gay man before and apparently he has taken it upon himself to give her a little education on all things gay – that's definitely his way. I'm sure she's gotten more than she bargained for.

When the weekend came, it was a different story. Without exaggeration, the nurse covering for Donna was beyond awful. First, I don't know that I've ever seen someone this unhealthy looking working as a nurse. By the time she got to the second landing of our building (the elevator was out), she was breathing so hard I was afraid she was going to collapse right in front of me. And her personality matched her physical appearance: largely unattractive.

I tried hard not to let her looks bother me; it was possible she was a competent nurse. Then I saw her work!

She didn't wear gloves, she just unwrapped needles, tubes, and whatever else she needed and dropped them around Stephan on the bed, and then she proceeded to use Stephan like a pincushion as she looked for a vein. I think she must have tried five different times before she was successful. On one attempt, a huge bubble of skin the size of an egg flared up around the needle and Stephan sat there wincing in pain. The next time, she missed the vein altogether and blood began dripping all over the bed. I was horrified, and REALLY pissed!

After she left, I told Stephan she was not allowed to come near him again. I also said if Stephan didn't make a complaint to her supervisor, I would. Stephan just sighed and said, "Maybe she's having a bad day." But I wouldn't let this one go. Finally, he said he would call.

I've taken a sick day today. My plan is to look at apartments and try to make some sense out of our finances. The dance studio wasn't all that complicated, but still, I don't know what it means to close a business, or how to do it.

As usual, our money situation is less than settled. We've completed Stephan's social security application. I heard on the radio that there is money immediately available for people with AIDS, so I got the application last week. I hope we'll get some help.

January 7

Everyone wants to know what they can do to help. I never have an answer for them. Or they say, "If you need anything, don't hesitate to call."

Call for what? What would I ask for? What do they know about AIDS and death? I know they mean well and they are truly concerned for us, but I don't know what to say or what to ask for.

Despite how tired Stephan has been, he managed to get himself together and look at apartments with me yesterday. He walked slowly and had to stop to catch his breath several times, but he stuck with it. The last place we looked at we decided was the one we wanted. It's in the Hoopskirt Factory on 3rd and Race. Huge windows, lots of light, hardwood floors, and a bedroom that sits in the back of the apartment, away from the living room. Stephan said, "That way, I can close the door if I don't want to see anyone."

I completed the application and paid the fee. We should know by tomorrow if the apartment is ours. If it is, we can move in this weekend.

Now, this is where we could use a little help: moving. Stephan's worried because I'm "doing too much," and I'm not getting a chance to relax. I know he's right but what am I supposed to do? A lot of things have to be taken care of, quickly. I decided to listen to Stephan and take another sick day tomorrow.

January 8

I had a dream last night about a woman having a baby and I was in the delivery room. The baby was delivered in a big bubble (I guess the water never broke). The woman fed the baby for a while. We named him John. Next thing I know I am on my parents' front lawn with the baby. Dad is driving away in the old family VW van and for some reason I didn't want him to think the baby was mine (at this point I realize that he is). I wrap the baby up and bring him over to our neighbor's house where the mother is living. I put the baby to bed and tell him I love him. He says he loves me too.

I've decided it's also time to look for a new job. I don't have the energy or emotional space to keep working as a therapist. More than once I have found myself sitting in family sessions wondering about Stephan or stifling my annoyance at the problems my clients came in to talk with me about. I need something that doesn't require so much emotional investment, something mindless and with a flexible schedule.

So once again, I'm looking at restaurant work. I submitted applications at the Four Seasons and The Rittenhouse along with other restaurants in town, but it doesn't look like anyone is hiring right now.

The doctor has stopped Stephan's IV treatment for pneumonia because his blood pressure has dropped so low. Now for the next five days Stephan's on two pills, which aren't making him feel too good.

I was talking with a friend about all the shit that's been happening in the last few weeks: we closed the dance studio and folded the dance company; I met with our landlord to discuss breaking our three-year lease after less than a year (he was incredibly supportive); I'm looking for a new job; I have to pack our stuff and get ready to move... not to mention all the stress around Stephan's health and medication issues. I started crying with those heavy, gut-punching sobs. I don't know how I'm going to get through this. While writing these words, I can feel this pain growing in my heart, and tears have begun falling.

All I want is peace.

January 9

Last night, I barely finished writing the word 'peace,' and I immediately fell into another crying jag that must have lasted 10 minutes. Then I walked over to the window ledge, lit a cigarette and looked for something in the world below to distract me for a while.

When I finally went to bed, Stephan was sleeping as usual. I crawled in next to him, surrounding myself in his warmth. It was delicious, soft, and wonderful. His breath was quiet and short, like a little baby. I moved in next to him and felt his whole body unfold like a quiet sigh. It was so comfortable. I began to unfold as well. For that brief moment, everything felt fine. We were warm, we were comfortable, and we had each other. There was something profound in this silence and I stayed awake to enjoy it as long as I could. As I lay there, I wondered if Stephan could feel this through the thin veil of sleep. I hoped he did; he would have liked it.

We got the okay on the apartment today, so when I got home from work, I grabbed a quick dinner and began packing things. I called about the electric, gas, and phone today, too. We'll be moving this weekend.

Everything is happening a little too fast for me, but I'm trying to keep myself focused on what has to get done. In typical Stephan fashion, this morning when we got up he said he has decided that he is not going to take the medication he was prescribed since stopping the IV treatment. It makes him feel "too weird."

There was no discussion, he wasn't asking for advice; he was simply letting me know what his decision was. I wasn't going to fight him on this, but I did suggest he speak to his doctor first. He said he'd think about it.

January 10

Every time I think I've seen Stephan at his worst, there comes another day where he looks more drained and pale. When I got home from work tonight, he was so depressed, it was really sad – and frightening. He said he couldn't stop his mind from these racing thoughts. He wonders if his health is going to get worse, what's he going to look like when he dies, am I going to leave him, how much more can he take, what is the rest of his life going to be like… All this stuff keeps running around in his mind.

I understood everything he was saying. The truth is, these are my thoughts (fears) too – all except the one about leaving him.

What do you say to someone who is staring at the end of his life? I tried to comfort him. Then, feeling useless, I kissed him and told him I'd go make us tea. It was the best I could do.

January 11

It's moving day today. We've got plenty of help. I'm sending Stephan over to a friend's house and we're just going to plow through it as quickly as possible.

Last night Stephan had a fever. It was up to 103. We're not sure why. I hope it's not another infection. He was emphatic last night that he sign his living will. It took a while but we found it. I can't even imagine what it must feel like for him. I said that to Stephan and he said he couldn't even figure out how to describe it. He's afraid of suffering too much and he is especially afraid of developing AIDS-related dementia.

Me, too.

It is the strangest thing, going through this whole experience. Anxiety and fear can run so high, I just feel myself looking for an out, some kind of release. I was lucky enough to get my hands on pot. So I have gotten high a few times over the past week. It doesn't make anything go away, but for a while I feel more relaxed. I've also noticed that I've been eating a lot of sweets, cakes, cookies, and junk. Another way of dealing with stress, I guess. Though it could also be munchies – I do love a good oatmeal cookie when I'm stoned.

Still, there are times when nothing can take away this bottomless worry. I move aimlessly from reading to watching TV to eating. Nothing can hold my attention. The only thing that really helps is to take a walk. As I walk through Old City and Society Hill, I let my thoughts roll out with the traffic. Sometimes my thoughts get the better of me, though, and I have to sit down because my tears have developed into an all-out cry. Other times, I just walk, sunglasses on, tears falling, breathing deeply.

January 12

I will say this; we have a fabulous apartment. This is the first time I've felt totally relaxed in my own living space in a long, long time. The 10-foot windows make it feel bright, clean, and warm. We are on the top floor, and there is an incredible view of the Ben Franklin Bridge from our living room windows, and the traffic below sounds like ocean waves rolling past us along 3rd St.. At night, when the High Speed line goes across the Ben Franklin Bridge to New Jersey, it triggers this sequence of lights that run up and down the cables.

Tonight, we had a little dinner and then sat on the sofa for a while, just enjoying the quiet. Everything felt so soft and easy. "I like our place," Stephan said. "It feels good." Then he kissed my forehead and said, "Thank you."

January 14

For the last few days, I've had this really short fuse. I suppose this is not too surprising. I've been trying to figure out what is going on, so I can deal with it, and this morning it hit me: Part of me is dying. Slowly, every day, a part of my heart is dying. And there is little I can do about it.

It doesn't matter what I do, how hard I work, how often I tell Stephan I love him; he is going to die, and with him will go a part of me. I don't know what to do about this anger. I hate him for being sick. I hate not being able to do anything. I also hate how isolated I feel with this. And I hate these words I've just written.

The other night, Stephan said, "I just want a little time to really enjoy our new place and each other." For some reason, I don't think that's going to happen. Stephan is still really tired and he's been running a pretty high fever. I'm sure he's got another infection.

Of course he didn't call the doctor. I think he's afraid of it actually being worse (kind of like his doctor confirming his worst fears).

Stephan said he'd call tomorrow. Maybe it's nothing.

January 17

I had a lot of trouble falling asleep last night. This is pretty unusual for me. It took me the better part of an hour to fall asleep after we had gone to bed. I just lay there and tried to concentrate on my breathing and the next thing I knew, I was trying to solve our money problems, or I'd hear Stephan's breathing and wonder if he's all right. I don't know how, but I finally gave up and fell asleep.

I've got the next four days off. The thing about this is that I need to let myself unwind and that is hard to do when Stephan is around. He can be so needy. Lately, I don't enjoy being around him. I try, but it just feels so heavy and frustrating.

I guess I'm angry – still (or again). He's sick, there's little we can do together, there's little I can get from him. So, I end up retreating into myself, even when we're together. It is so hard to accept what is happening. There is no future. It leaves me continually uneasy.

January 18

We've been here for a week. Slowly, it's beginning to feel like a home for us—the furniture is in the right place, the boxes are gone, and we have artwork on the walls. There is a certain stability that is coming together, which leaves me both hopeful and anxious. I know sooner or later things will change.

Stephan went to the doctors yesterday. They ran the usual tests and X-rays and found everything to be okay. It seems that much of what Stephan has been feeling (the fatigue, the temperatures) is just the virus doing what the virus does.

Stephan said that for the first time yesterday, he realized he's never going to feel the way he did before. All this time he was waiting for his body to return to normal and it's hit him that it won't. There was a sad acceptance in his voice. I know this is not an easy thing to come to terms with. He's got this noble manner, though, and said he's just got to get used to the fact that some days are not going to feel good.

So, I guess we're both struggling with acceptance.

I've filled out more applications for waiter positions at a couple of hotels in the city. I'm hoping to be out of my counseling job soon; it's really getting to be too much.

Yesterday, after one of my clients said something about feeling suicidal, all hell broke loose. I had to cancel the rest of my appointments and organize an emergency psych evaluation, which was like trying to herd a group of cats. The parents were resistant, the psychiatrist on duty was a pain in the ass, and the paperwork was unbelievable!

Then I had to come home and deal with Stephan and all the stuff going on here. If I don't find another job soon, I think I'll explode.

I haven't told anyone in my family that we've moved yet. Of course, this is only adding to the tension and stress I feel. If I tell them we moved, do I also talk about Stephan's diagnosis, or can I hide that a little longer? Does it even matter if I tell them about moving? No one comes to visit. I could be in the middle of North Dakota somewhere and it wouldn't really make much difference.

January 19

There are times when I can't stop thinking about what life will be like without Stephan. Hundreds of different scenarios play themselves out in my mind. Sometimes I feel incredibly sad, and other times I am very much at peace and find warmth in different memories.

But then, Stephan calls me from the bedroom and I go in to find him soaked in sweat. Calmly I take his temperature and bring him some juice and aspirin.

During these times, it's not so easy and serene. I fight back tears and stroke his worried face. "That was a pretty bad one," he says. "Like when there's an especially loud clap of thunder." I say, "Yeah baby, I guess it was," and pull up the blanket.

January 20

For two nights in a row, Stephan has awakened around 3:30 A.M. with the chills. His whole body just shaking, even though he was buried way under the covers. He'd been running a low-grade fever all day. I fixed him some tea each time and gave him some aspirin. Eventually, he went back to sleep, huddled close to me for warmth. I pulled his arms around me and fell asleep sending him warm, loving thoughts.

This morning when I took his temperature, the fever was gone. He sighed from under the covers and said, "That was a hell of a battle."

January 21

This morning I told Stephan I loved him, as I say quite often, and he asked, "What does that mean?" I didn't have an answer. I still don't.

I can't explain what or why I feel. The strange thing is that the "love" feeling, that head over heels, walking on air feeling, has faded. Love now seems a matter of commitment and respect.

We haven't had sex in so long I almost forget what it feels like. Our lives have shifted into this weird kind of longing. Everything has changed and we're just following this ugly path, wishing the scenery would change.

So, why do I love Stephan? Because I do. Three years ago, I was given an open invitation to be with him and I stepped in willingly. Had I known what was in store for me, I think I still would have joined him.

Still haven't done anything about telling my family about our move. Every time I think about it, I get nervous and imagine how I explain it. I'm so tired of lying – but to tell the truth? I'm too tired to try and deal with whatever fallout comes from finally saying that Stephan has AIDS.

And… I'm very aware that in not telling them, I can just fan the quiet fire of anger and resentment. As tired as the anger game gets, I haven't figured out how to quit.

January 31

We now keep a supply of towels by the bed because Stephan's night sweats are so bad. Even though the doctor has prescribed something, Stephan still wakes up two or three times a night completely soaked. He said, "It's the worst feeling, to lay there and just feel this sweat dripping off you. Then you wake up and try to figure out what to do with the top sheet which is now soaked. So are my pillow and my head. So you finally get yourself together – put on a robe and put a towel across the pillow. The you lay back down only to go through the same thing again in an hour." The doctor suggested doubling the amount of medicine to see if it makes a difference.

We'll see.

I've finally written to Mom and Dad. I realized that holding on to this anger wasn't helping and just kept me at a distance, feeling resentful. So, I started by thinking about what it was that connected me to them. I decided to begin the note by thanking them for what they had given me – and suddenly my tears flowed with my words. I told them how much I respected them, their relationship, even their faith. I said they showed me what love and commitment are. I told them I knew how much they loved me, how important their love was to me. And as I was writing, I realized what it was I had to do.

My next sentence began, "I want you to know that I forgive you."

I had to stop writing and sob for a bit, really consider what I'd written. It was true – I had to forgive them. They would never be the parents I wanted. They could only be who they are. I had to let go of what I never really had (open, accepting parents)… and figure out how to be okay with what I was given.

I continued, "I understand how and why your faith guides you. Where I was wrong

19

was to hope for more from you and your faith – and then to get angry when you couldn't respond the way I wanted. And for that, I ask your forgiveness."

I don't expect a whole lot to change from sending the letter, at least not in terms of my family's involvement in my life and their openness to Stephan. Still, it helped to take a minute and recognize how my parents are contributing to my life, even if they don't know the complete story.

It's pretty clear to me that I am able to stay within this whole experience with Stephan because of the love and commitment they not only modeled for me, but gave me, as well. I am so grateful for this contribution (and for many others). I know Stephan and his family are, as well.

They still don't know about his diagnosis, though. God knows what that letter will say.

ONE OF ELEVEN

I have ten siblings, and one of them is a fraternal twin brother. We grew up in a five-bedroom house in the suburbs of Philadelphia, in a neighborhood with optimistic farm-themed streets like Grayhorse Road and Windmill Ave. My family's house was on Red Barn, a three-block stretch of road that lay at bottom of the county's highest hill.

My home sat in the middle of a small valley. Surrounded by hills I raced bikes with friends up and down the streets of our neighborhood all summer, and sled down snow-packed paths behind the houses in winter. We had a fairly big backyard, dominated by a huge maple that shaded most of the yard, including the swing set at the bottom of the hill. Beyond that rusty, creaky old swing set, there were three acres of woods filled with thin birches clustered in little groves surrounded by towering large oak and maple. There is a dirt trail that snakes away from the edge of our yard and ends at a small creek where we splashed around, hunting for crayfish and frogs in the humid summer months. There was also an old, broken down stone building not far down the creek from our house that we used as "headquarters" to countless imagined adventures when we were children.

Usually, when people hear about the size of my family, there is an initial shock, followed by a reflexive, nod and the words, "Irish Catholic?" burped out in a knowing tone that offers both condolence and respect. I'm used to this response, I understand what the tone implies; the unimaginable challenges of growing up in a home where faith was fundamental and space was minimal.

Still, I need to be very clear. I had a great childhood filled with everything a little boy would want. I was loved, taken good care of, and always had friends and siblings around to play with. At night, I'd fall asleep listening

21

to the endless song of the crickets and the rolling waves of the night breezes weaving through the maple tree in our backyard. And every night, somewhere deep in the distance, past the woods and across the valley, there was a steady, rolling rhythm that pulled at my attention. CLICK-CLICK…click-click.

Two miles away, at the very edge of town, freight trains rode nightly from center city Philadelphia out past the different towns of Montgomery and Bucks county. I could hear their wheels rolling across the tracks in a steady rhythm CLICK-CLICK… click-click… CLICK-CLICK… click-click… CLICK-CLICK… Every night, I closed my eyes and rode those trains to far-away places, having secret adventures only young boys can know.

When I stop and think about how my parents raised us, I can't help but be amazed, and very appreciative. They would be the first to tell you that their secret was being organized – about everything. Mom used to say, "I broke the house work up into floors."

Monday, she stripped the beds and washed the linens on the third floor. Tuesdays, it was the second floor. Wednesdays, she cleaned the living room and dining room. Thursdays, it was the kitchen. In between the house cleaning, Mom also had to take care of the endless supply of dirty diapers put out from the 1-3 kids under the age of three, plus the clothes that eleven children went through on a daily basis. And of course, she prepared three meals each day and while getting dinner ready, supervised homework of 3-5 kids at the kitchen table.

Still, every night at five-thirty, Mom would stop what she was doing and say to whoever was in the kitchen, "I'm going upstairs run a comb through my hair before your father gets home, keep an eye on the stove." Ten minutes later, she was back, hair in place, and blotting a fresh coat of lipstick with a tissue.

My mother was the original energizer bunny, constantly in motion, and, for 13 years of her life, she was pregnant. She was a tiny little thing, too, maybe 5'1". She swore she was 5' 2", but we all knew better. The priests in our parish always shook their heads when they saw our family coming, smiling they'd remind us Mom was "sainted woman."

My mother grew up the youngest of five in north Philly. When her brother and sisters came to visit, Uncle Jim always had the guitar and banjo with him. After sending the kids to bed, the adults would all sit around the living room, smoking cigarettes and drinking Manhattans, singing these crazy, old songs for hours. Some of us would sneak out of bed and lie at the top of the steps listening to "Lida Rose" or "Sweet and Low" in four-part harmony, trying not to get caught. We'd lie there in our pajamas until we fell asleep and were carried back to our rooms in a thin fog of whiskey and cigarette smoke.

When she was younger, Mom took singing lessons. She had a great voice, and liked to sing as she moved through the house from room to room. One of my favorite memories of her happened one evening after dinner. My siblings and I are all playing outside after dinner. I am hiding behind the pine tree that sits outside the kitchen window trying so hard not to get caught that at first I don't notice Mom at the sink. Then she starts to sing, and for the briefest moment, time stopped. All I could hear was her voice floating sweetly into the yard, effortless, graceful, and content. I was so distracted by her singing, the tone of her voice, that I didn't even notice my brother come up and tag me, sending me to "jail," where I would have to wait for someone to set me free.

And Dad? Well, he was the oldest of three and grew up in West Philly. Things were a little rough in his home, stemming from his father's gambling and drinking problems, which eventually led to divorce. We didn't see as much of Dad's family growing up, and there was definitely no singing when they did come to visit.

Dad graduated from Villanova with a degree in chemical engineering, and found work in water waste management right out of college. He was also a mathematician, and at some point in my younger years, he took on a second job teaching math and advanced calculus two nights a week at LaSalle College in Philadelphia.

He was more than just a good provider; Dad knew how to stretch a dollar, and his logical, ordered approach to things provided a good counter-balance to my mom's more emotional and sentimental nature. Every morning, he kissed my mother's cheek on his way out the door to work wearing his white shirt and tie, the scent of Old Spice lingering behind. When he'd come home at night, he'd offer the same chaste kiss, and dinner would be served.

Dad's weekends were spent working around the house or rounding up as many of the kids as possible and taking us out for a "special trip" so that Mom could have some time to herself. Those special trips have become some my best memories of my father. I can still see him slowly walking along the Bryn Athen train tracks on a Sunday afternoon, humming as five or six of us scampered around him like a bunch of puppies.

Another special trip was when Dad did the Friday night food shopping. He'd pile a bunch of us into the back of the old VW bus and we'd ride over to the A&P, singing songs or playing some game to entertain us on the way to and from. Even our neighborhood friends would join us – food shopping with the Connells was something to experience! Four carts manned by kids scurrying around the store searching for whatever item my father assigned. He, in the meantime, would stroll up and down the aisles with the youngest tucked into the seat of his cart, whistling and crossing things off the list my mother made.

Organization was one of my parents' best tools for raising a big family. Knowing the value of a dollar was another. Some of Dad's better money saving ideas included an arrangement with the bakery department at the A&P to buy their day old bread at a reduced rate (we went through more than 12 loaves of bread a week). My parents bought a separate freezer just for the bread Dad bought. Dad also learned how to butcher chickens because it was less expensive to buy them whole. Every Friday night, after the groceries were put away, he'd put the chickens on the counter (6-8 of them), sharpen the best knife we had, and get to work.

We never drank whole milk growing up. Instead, Dad saved money by going to Weinrich's Bakery in the center of town, and purchasing a 50-pound bag of powdered milk from Mr. Weinrich. I can still see Dad heaving the big brown bag into the back of the bus and seeing a small cloud of smoke rise around the edges. At home, every night, it was one of the children's jobs to blend six pitchers of milk and put them in the fridge for the next day.

The one money-saving project that Dad took on none of the boys liked was his Home Barber Kit from Sears. Once a month, we lined up on the patio and Dad buzzed our hair down to the scalp. We dreaded our monthly cuts, and knew they were completely unavoidable. To this day, the sound of clippers snapping causes me to wince.

But those tense moments were far and few between. Mostly, I thought of our family as this weird hybrid of The Brady Bunch and The Waltons, complete with nights where we could call to each other from our beds at night.

"Good Night, Jim Bob," I'd shout from the room I shared with two of my brothers. And my sister would giggle from the third floor, "Good Night, Mary Ellen." But this is where The Connells diverge from the wholesome goodness of a TV family. From the third floor, one of my older brothers would rip a loud fart, then another, setting the whole house screaming and laughing. My mother through her own laughter would try to calm us down.

And there, in the middle of our growing, energetic family, was the Catholic faith. In many ways, it was the twelfth, and favored, child. During our younger years, none of it really mattered. Church and faith were just part of everything else. We said grace before and kept a huge copy of the Bible on the coffee table in the living room. There was mass on Sundays and holy days, and, of course, all the children went through 12 years of Catholic schooling.

Did I truly believe in what I was being taught? I suppose I did, as much as any boy of six or seven believes what his parents and teachers tell him. My idea of faith at that age involved sin and a lot of standing and kneeling. In our home, faith also seemed to mean crucifixes – lots of them. In every room, God's dying son stared at you with blank eyes, constantly suffering for your sins.

Still, these were the things our parents believed, and that was good enough for us – for the time being, anyway. I don't think any of us liked going to Confession or coming in from playing on Good Friday to say the rosary with our mother from noon to three (when Jesus was on the cross). But we were Irish Catholics; a bit of suffering is good for the soul (whatever that meant).

The wheels of faith were set in motion; my siblings and I simply rode along trusting our parents. Besides, how hard was it, really? I did my penance and imagined scrubbing the black spots of sin off my soul, gave up meat for Lent, memorized whatever we were told in Religion class. None of it was especially difficult. As long as I could get outside and ride my bike or go play in the woods behind our house, I was set.

It wasn't until later, when our family shifted into the rough waters of adolescence, that our lives began to change. By then, when I heard those freight trains hauling goods away in the night, I'd ride into other worlds where I had freedom and the independence I was denied at home. I listened to those wheels clicking along the tracks offering quiet words of advice, "NOT-YET… just wait… NOT-YET… just-wait…."

AIDS Timeline #2

In 1984, two scientists were working to discover what causes AIDS, Luc Montagnier (Pasteur Institute, France) and Robert Gallo (National Institute of Health, US); both claimed they had discovered the HIV virus. Montagnier was eventually credited with the discovery of the virus that causes AIDS, HIV (Human Immunodeficiency Virus).

By December 31, 1984, 11,055 people have been diagnosed with AIDS in the US, 5,620 have died from the disease.

The first AIDS related play on Broadway, Larry Kramer's "The Normal Heart" opened April 21, 1985.

June 30, 1985, Ryan White, a teenager with AIDS (through contaminated blood treatment) is barred from school in Kokomo, Indiana.

October, 1985, The First International Conference in AIDS is held in Atlanta, hosted by the US Department of Health and Human Services and the World Health Organization.

February 7

Stephan remains depressed. Nothing stimulates him. He has to make himself get out of bed and do things. I try to offer advice or suggestions but he has a reason why each of them wouldn't work. His stomach is upset because of the medicine, he's feeling worthless, he's not eating well, and he still sweats at night. All this would make even a saint feel a little lethargic; I guess he's entitled to a being in a funk.

What makes it hard for me is that I have become the one person that makes him feel better. He literally waits by the door until I come home from work. Then, in the evening he wants to spend every minute with me. If I go to the kitchen for something, he asks, "Where you going?" Most of the time, it's not so bad. We're just sitting, watching TV or holding hands as we talk. Still… it's also hard to write and work on any of my goals when he's constantly asking for my attention.

"My spirit is dying," he said a few nights ago in the dark of our bedroom. I didn't know what to say or do, so I sat there and fought back my tears. This is one of the saddest things I have ever heard him say, and I can see why he's saying it.

How do I get Stephan to see the benefit of getting angry and screaming or crying? He's spending all this energy on keeping it in control and he is smothering his spirit in the process. I get so angry I want to shake him, just so he'll feel something and share it, free himself a little. It's all too threatening (and frightening) for him, though.

Every time I come home and find him in bed, watching TV, he's a little less vibrant a little more gone. He's stuck, and I feel like I can't reach him any more.

Last night, Stephan was up four times because of his sweating. The last time, I got up, too, because I felt him just sitting up, not moving, and not doing anything. When I asked what was wrong, he mumbled something about being wet and not knowing what to do. I grabbed some towels and got him dried off again. As I have seen so many times before, he was like a child, confused and helpless, wondering what was happening around him.

I fucking hate it.

February 15

"Ask me to, I will give my world to you baby."

I went to see Patti LaBelle last night with Stephan's sister. Stephan was supposed to go, too, but he couldn't get it together. He loves Miss Patti. We saw her in concert a few years ago; it was one of the best shows I'd ever seen. Last night, when Miss Patti sang the words to "If You Ask Me To," something in me opened up. I couldn't stop crying. I felt like she was singing those words to me, for me. I sat in my seat, a crying mess. The show was great. Stephan would have enjoyed it. I missed him during the whole performance.

Reality is beginning to sink in for me, in a hard, heavy way. There isn't going to be any remission for Stephan. No chance to "do everything" before IT returned. IT was here.

Yesterday I took a sick day (again) and went with Stephan to the doctor. For the past two days, he's been running a fever of 103 or more. His stomach has been bloated and he knows something is wrong. The good news is that his lungs are nice and clear. The bad news is the doctor didn't know what was going on with Stephan's stomach.

Stephan was given the choice of going into the hospital for a few tests or taking care of them on an outpatient basis. Not surprisingly, he chose to get them done as an outpatient. This Monday, he goes to see an ophthalmologist. There is some concern about a blood test, something about the presence (or lack of) CMV, which may indicate retinitis. I don't completely get it. I just shook my head.

Then on Thursday, Stephan is getting a CAT scan on his abdomen. Should things begin to feel worse before all this is done, Stephan just has to call and he will be admitted.

He won't call.

February 20

It's been a difficult couple of days. Stephan's been irritable and bitchy. It seems like anything I do is not done the way he likes it, or quickly enough. Something as simple as getting the wrong flavor of juice sets him off on an evil mood that won't go away for hours.

I understand none of this is directed at me personally. I understand Stephan is dealing with a lot of different emotions, which can be scary. Still, his anger hurts me. It hurts because I can't do anything to make this go away. It hurts because sometimes, loving someone is not enough. And it hurts because I feel so alone.

Sooner or later, it all catches up with me and I find myself crying and sobbing on the sofa. Rocking back and forth, eyes closed, I cry and cry until I am too tired to continue. Or I'll duck behind the dining room table, and sit on the floor with a towel in my mouth so Stephan can't hear, and let the tears and sobs shake my body until I am completely spent.

Last night, after one of these crying sessions, I got ready for bed, climbed in next to Stephan and kissed him. "I love you." I said. A thin line of tears traced his cheek and he said, "I don't get it. I've been such an asshole. People I've known don't stay around like this." I kissed him again and said, "That's not me."

February 25

When I got home last night, Stephan was not feeling well. He was really warm and tired. He kept saying, "I want to go home now. You understand. I know you do." And I did.

He looked tired – tired and frightened. I held his hand and cried those tears that are now too familiar. This morning, Stephan's fever was still high – over 103. I called the doctor and he said we should come in. Stephan and I both knew what this meant: he was being readmitted.

We took care of whatever paperwork was necessary and left the doctor's office. On our way to admissions, Stephan broke down. Right outside the elevators he started crying so hard it scared me. I held him as close as I could, my tears and sobs joining his. People were walking past us, trying to get off or on the elevator, but it didn't matter. We were stuck in that space, holding onto each other, looking for the strength to keep going.

No one is sure what is wrong, other than there is an infection. There will be tests and labs completed over the next few days.

February 28

I took the day off and slept until ten, when I was awakened by a phone call from Stephan's sister. She said Stephan had had a seizure this morning and was under medication so he couldn't talk. I don't know anything else. I hope he wasn't by himself, and that the nurses were good to him. I'm sure it scared him. I wonder what this means. Has the virus entered his nervous system? Will it happen again?

The last time I saw Stephan was yesterday afternoon. The medication he was taking made him nauseous and I watched as he forced himself to eat chicken and rice. He said, "If you eat it fast, it goes down easier."

It's now after midnight and I'm too wired to sleep. I went to the gym and then over to the hospital. Stephan looked absolutely horrible. He had an oxygen tube in his nose, he was breathing fast and was feverish again.

Most of the afternoon, I watched him sleep and tried to get some rest myself. Every so often, Stephan would wake up for a few minutes. He'd try to talk and asked the same question, "When did you get here?" I guess they gave him pretty potent drugs.

By late afternoon, he was a little more together. I bathed him, changed his gown, and he tried to eat dinner. I also snuck a look at his chart. From what I could figure out, none of the tests had turned up anything. The seizure this morning is still a mystery. Stephan was scheduled for a CAT scan, an EKG, and an MRI to make sure everything was okay.

The evening nurse seems to think that Stephan's seizure was a reaction to the medication he was taking. She said he really didn't seize but arched his back and some other things indicative of a bad reaction to medication. I tried to understand what she was saying but missed some of it. The good thing is the neurologist is in agreement.

February 29

I got up at around 8:00 this morning. Kind of early for a Saturday but I couldn't sleep. I know what people mean when they describe their house as feeling empty. That's what our apartment feels like. I putzed around for a while; trying to convince myself I could handle being by myself. After all, I'd done it before. This time feels different, though.

I made coffee, fixed breakfast, and pretended it wasn't so bad. I suppose it really was okay – I survived. Still, there was this undercurrent of pain that seemed to pull at my body. Thankfully, it grew close to 11:00 and I left for the hospital. Meltdown avoided.

Stephan seemed much better today. He was still tired, but I walked in to find him doing some "exercises" in bed (pulling his knee to his chest). He's afraid of looking like "one of them," the AIDS victims – all worn and withered from the disease. So he worked his legs a little and then I bathed him.

He looked at me as I washed him and asked if he had lost his dignity. What could I say? He was still beautiful to me.

There are times when I feel like I'm still waiting for my mind to catch up with my body. I'm doing everything I'm supposed to: the cats are fed, bills are paid, and I go to work. Somewhere in the middle of this, I visit Stephan at the hospital. Once again, I feel like I am watching myself as I go through all this. It's not like others don't help or that I don't ask (which has come surprisingly easy lately). But even when this happens, I'm a voyeur watching myself do what I should.

I never noticed how much I relied on my relationship with Stephan. He has become a part of who I am, and his absence is as obvious to me as when you remove a ring that you've worn forever. I wish I could know how much longer we had – he had. He was talking so confidently this afternoon, like he would be home in a few days. As bad as it sounds, I got anxious. It struck me: He will be coming home. We're not finished yet. We're far from finished. I wanted to yell at him, "What's the fucking point! Can't we just stop everything now, please?!"

Instead, I kissed his forehead and held his hand and tried to think about what would need to happen if he were to return home. Should I take a leave of absence? Can I get a schedule of people to stay with him while I'm at work? What if he really bounces back from this? How do I set things up at home? Who can I call? Can I get through this?

March 2

I spoke with Stephan's doctor today. Whatever MAI is, that's what Stephan is being treated for. I think it's some kind of infection that they treat the same way as tuberculosis. Stephan is taking four different medicines for this, plus AZT, Demerol and Prozac. On top this; he has something to help him sleep at night. He's a fucking one-man pharmacy.

I stopped by to see Stephan today for about half an hour. He just came back from his EEG. On my way, I was thinking about how much time Stephan is by himself and I wondered what it must feel like to be going through all these different tests alone. For his part, Stephan was simply annoyed. He wasn't getting much rest and he was tired, as usual. He said to me, "If one of our cats showed the same kinds of physical symptoms I am, they'd be put to sleep. Why do people have to be so helpful?"

He had a point.

When I got home, there was a message on the answering machine. I've been offered a waiter position at a restaurant in town. Finally!

So now I'm faced with all the details associated with leaving my job. I have to write a letter of resignation, give four weeks' notice, and terminate with all my clients. Change has become a constant part of my life, and, in many ways, leaving this job doesn't have any of the sadness or anxiety it might under different circumstances — at least, not yet.

I don't know what to do about telling my family about all of this. They still don't know about Stephan's diagnosis, how do I tell them that I've quit my job? I'll have to think about this one.

So, here I am, at the age of thirty, returning to work in a restaurant. I thought once I got my Master's Degree, I'd never have to do this again.

ABOUT BEING A TWIN

It's always been difficult for me to talk about being a twin. Not because of difficult emotions or experiences – though there are plenty of both, I suppose. It's difficult because it is layered within a larger family context that I think neutralized some of the uniqueness of sharing a birthday (and a womb).

There are eleven children in our family; my twin brother (Tim) is number seven, which makes me lucky number eight. By the time we came along, it was already a very busy scene, with my parents in constant motion keeping us fed, clothed, clean, and most of all, loved.

Whenever we'd talk about those early years in the family, our mother liked to remind us that this was back when there were no disposable diapers. And at one point in her career as a mother, she had 4 children in diapers! I can still see (and smell) that old diaper pail sitting by the big soapstone washtub in the laundry room.

Back then, we were frequently referred to as "The Twins," but it often didn't matter that we WERE twins. It was a moniker, really, easier than saying both our names. And when you consider we are fraternal, with dispositions that are polar opposites, whatever "twinness" we have is filtered even more. In many ways, as twins go, my brother Tim and I are as different as can be. I always tell people, that he looks like my mothers' side of the family. I am, so I've been told, the spitting image of my father. At least that's what one of my aunts said to me, her hands resting on my cheeks as she pressed my face away from her, adjusting the distance a few times until she could see me without her bifocals.

Tim definitely favored Mom's side of the family. Shorter stature, a little thicker in the trunks and legs, he was always "more Wilson than Connell," as our Grandmother would say. But it's not just our looks that set us apart, from the beginning, we moved through the world very differently. The story goes, that after Tim was born, the doctor turned to the nurses and instructed them to "finish up." I like how Mom told the story, her face, and the inflection in her voice. We've heard it a million times at the dinner table, "I turned to the doctor and said, 'I don't think I'm finished yet' and 8 minutes later, Terry was born – feet first."

And there it was: Tim, out in front, making noise, already the performer. And me, taking my time, my feet under me, a little removed from the rest of the action. No one even knew I was coming….until the very last minute. Mom always shrugged and said something like, "I guess you were hidden behind your brother." I like that I came out feet first. It's a bit of comfort to think I was already on my way to something.

There are a few cute stories from our childhood that make the rounds whenever the family gets together and begins the "how 'bouts". When we were around two, and Mom wanted us to get outside for a little fresh air, things got a little more complicated. As toddlers, we certainly couldn't be left out on our own. But by this time, our younger brother Patrick was born, and there was the endless mountain of laundry, lunch to clean up from, dinner to make… Mom's solution was to get two harnesses, connect them to a few yards of rope, all tied to a stake Dad hammered into the ground. In other words, she put us on leashes.

Mom liked to tell the story about getting us ready to go out. She'd cover her mouth and laugh, saying, "I'd sit you both up on the dryer, turn around to get the harnesses off their hooks, and when I'd turn back, there you'd be with your arms out (she holds her arms in front of her like she was sleep walking and lifts here eyebrows sadly), the two of you, waiting to be zipped in." Mom said she hated the harnesses; worrying one of the neighbors would call the police on her for "treating her children like dogs." It would be one of the thousands of little things she suffered as a mother. I imagine her saying a Hail Mary as she looked out the kitchen window into the back yard, where two of her children sat next to each other on the ground, tethered to a metal hook.

But she underestimated us. We were Connells, after all, children of an engineer. Not a week after my brother and I were put into those harnesses, we learned how to get each other out of them. "I was in the kitchen, getting lunch ready and this time when I looked out, all I saw was a pair of empty harnesses on the ground. Kidnapped! That's all I kept could think…. from our own back yard! I ran out the kitchen door, calling your names. When I looked to the right, there the two of you were, waddling around in your diapers in the Geiger's backyard two houses away, not a care in the world."

There's another story from when we were infants when my family used to stage the Table Races, watching to see who'd get from one end of the kitchen table to the other first. My brothers and sisters were hooting and laughing as Tim and I were put at one end of the table and were encouraged to make our way to the other – the first of countless competitions we'd endure throughout our lives. And somehow, somewhere, the story got tagged with the ending "…and Timmy always won because Terry would stop for a piece of food."

Tim likes to hear the story about him trying to climb up onto the couch. He says it typifies the differences between us. We were toddlers, learning how to walk, propelling ourselves drunkenly from one piece of furniture to another. One night after dinner, the adults were sitting in the living room with coffee (and cigarettes, I'm sure). Tim and I were playing in front of them, and at some point, I walked over to the couch, and with very little effort, climbed up and nestled into my grandmother's side. Tim sees this, and decided he wanted to do the same. He waddled over to the opposite side of the couch and tried repeatedly to get up. "With those chunky little legs of yours, you just couldn't reach," Mom would say, shaking her head, and always the hand covering her mouth, stifling a laugh, "but you kept on trying. Then, you decided to walk down to the other end of the couch and try there, thinking it might be easier where Terry had climbed up – which sent Grand Dad into stitches. There you were, doing the same dance (and the laughter gets harder to control), poor thing. Built like his grandfather. All the adults sat around roaring with laughter watching. Grand Dad thought it was one of the funniest things he had ever seen."

While it goes without saying, having a twin meant there was always someone to play with. But the thing is, in a family as big as ours, that idea was a bit redundant. In fact, there was always more than one person to play with. Tim and I spent our childhood years with at least one or two of our other siblings around when we were playing. If we were out in the neighborhood, it was usually three or four Connells with our friends, the same group of kids, day in, and day out.

If you ask me, getting away from everyone was the biggest challenge. Often, I'd grab my Hardy Boys book, my older brother's Boy Scout flashlight, and hide in our bedroom closet reading. If I heard someone calling me from the yard, or downstairs, I'd shut off the flashlight and sit perfectly still, hoping I wouldn't be caught. Other times, I'd sneak away to hike by myself into the woods, looking for fossils or rocks for my collection.

While we were constant companions as kids, our parents made sure that we were placed in different homeroom classes at school. In many ways, from the ages of 5 to 11 or 12, being a twin in our family didn't mean very much. There was a much larger group that dominated our world and took it over. We just went along for the ride, and at least from my point of view, it was a pretty good ride.

Except when it came to haircuts.

I can distinctly remember one time, when Tim was in the chair for his haircut. He was making all kinds of noise, crying, complaining, squirming the whole time and there was Dad, barely holding onto his patience. What was most striking about this particular moment was becoming aware of the fact that it didn't matter what Tim did... all the noise in the world wouldn't get him a better haircut. And in that moment, it occurred to me that it didn't make sense to struggle. It was better, because it was easier, to just follow the rules.

For me, the haircuts became just part of the package. Go to church, say our prayers, do our homework, get a haircut... None of it was especially difficult. Some of it was boring and didn't make much sense to me (church), but I basically did as I was told. Tim on the other hand would always scream, "That's not fair!" His catch phrase was, "But why?"

In my mind, if there were some time or place that typified who we were as twins, I'd have to say it was when we played house. Simply put, Tim was one of those little boys who liked to put on women's clothes, especially shoes. Always the performer, Tim would play the mother, leaving the true female in the cast, our sister Kathleen, to be one of the daughters. If we played school, Tim's teacher could be strict or kind, but always wore a dress and earing and perched her books on his right hip. If playing the principal, he wore pearls and gloves.

I don't remember my parents or the rest of the family reacting one way or another to it. Not that it would have mattered. If told little boys don't wear high heels, he would have responded with a resounding, "But Why?!"

My role, when playing house? I was the family dog! I would lick hands and roll over on command. Obedient, loved, just one of the gang. That was me. It was certainly who I tried to be.

And, that was us. Tim – pushing boundaries, out in front, directing the action, playing to the crowd; me taking things in, doing what I'm told, not interested in making waves, just interested in having fun.

We weren't the most boyish of boys, especially when it came to sports. And here, I think having a twin actually made it easier, especially when moving through the inevitable childhood rites of passage known as Little League. Every summer, we shared the role of worst player on the team. I couldn't imagine taking on Little League by myself.

We also went through Cub Scouts together, but things were a little more social and easier to navigate in this setting. Still we huddled next to each other and watched any time the rougher play of our "Pack" members started, and survived together, half heartedly whittling our cars for the Pinewood Derby or pretending to have fun during trips to a sporting event.

Always having Tim around, being a twin, it was all just part of a bigger picture that looked and felt good to me. It wasn't until we moved into sixth grade (adolescence), and the need for some sense of individuation took over, that being a twin became more of a problem.

AIDS Timeline #3

The surgeon general called for AIDS education for children of all ages and urged widespread use of condoms, <u>May, 1986</u>.

<u>September 19, 1986</u>, AZT, the first drug used to treat AIDS, begins clinical trials.

<u>October, 1986</u>, The Surgeon General's Report on Acquired Immune Deficiency Syndrome is released. This is the first, and only, national mailing of its kind.

By the <u>end of 1986</u>, AIDS cases have been reported on every continent in the world. In the U.S., there are 42,255 people diagnosed with AIDS, 24,699 have died.

<u>February 1987</u>, Burrough Wellcome (now known as Glaxo-SmithKline) announces the price of AZT at $10,000 per year, making AZT the most expensive drug in history.

<u>Published in 1987</u>, "And the Band Played On: Politics, People and the AIDS Epidemic," by Randy Shilts follows the discovery and spread of AIDS.

March 3

I got a call yesterday morning at 8:00; it was Stephan saying he was being discharged. I was NOT ready for this, especially because the day before, he was experiencing a strange, involuntary rocking motion with his head (which turned out to be anxiety). By noon I was at the hospital with a friend's car to pick him up.

Stephan had had two blood transfusions earlier in the day and he looked 100% better. I was warned, though, that transfusions are a tease. He would look and sound good for a few days, and then, when the effects wore off, he'd be tired and drawn again.

Stephan's doctor had reviewed everything with us. Some of the medications were being discontinued (AZT, two of the four antibiotics), DDI would be prescribed instead. Many results from different tests would not be back for at least a week. It was possible that the MAI Stephan was being treated for was not even present – that remained to be seen. In fact, it is now a consideration that Stephan has lymphoma. (Stephan already stated if he did have this, he was not going to have any treatments for it.)

As far as the fevers and sweats, little more could be done than was already prescribed. The whole way home, I didn't say anything. Stephan asked if I was angry with him for coming home. Of course I wasn't, not really. I was just angry. And worried. How long will all this go on? How many trips will we be taking to the hospital, fearing (and hoping) it was the last one? How much more of this could I take? What does it take for someone (Stephan) to say they've had enough?

Last night, Stephan spoke about how he had hit bottom this time, and he realized how much of his own power he had given up. He was tired and weak but decided he was going to "get his life back." He said he wasn't being dramatic, just making an attempt to be less negative. He also said he didn't want to fight this; rather, he was accepting what had happened. He was now ready to look at his life instead of his death. Then he asked if I would help him.

What could I say? The truth is I couldn't trust anything he said - especially when it came to getting better. Things won't ever get back to normal. Still, I told Stephan I believed he wanted to make things better for himself and I would support him as best I could. He doesn't need to know what my fears are – he has his own. I will let time do what it may and be with Stephan. Period.

Today, Stephan made himself eat breakfast and took a walk around the apartment a few times. It's shocking how weak he is. He continued his positive talk today.

He said, "Everything starts from an idea. 'Slaves' was an idea, our studio, your writing – everything. We can make a reality called 'being sick,' or we can make something completely different... one of life."

I understand his words but I am having a hard time believing them. I am hesitant to trust anything. I am trying to keep my expectations simple. I don't know what will happen, or when. Stephan's words are true, but I don't know who he's trying to convince – himself or me.

March 5

It was too good to last. Stephan had a real bad night. He was up at least four times changing towels and drying himself off. Then he got too worried to sleep (he didn't want to sweat again). My guess is that the transfusions have worn off and his body is back to its weak self.

This morning he was frustrated and tired, and a little worried. He kept saying, "I don't know what I'm going to do. I don't know what I'm going to do." We both ended up holding each other and crying for quite a while. I rocked Stephan back and forth in my arms, hushing him. I said, "I know you're tired, baby. You've been working real hard. Everything will be okay." I tried to soothe him (and myself).

It's unnerving seeing Stephan so emotional. I was glad to see him let go a little, but it broke my heart to see him so fragile and confused. This is the man who was always so sure of himself, and what he wanted in life. Eventually, we fell asleep, only to wake up a while later. Stephan was soaked in sweat again.

I've just checked in on him, it's now 10:30 pm. I checked the towels. They were wet again. I changed them and Stephan stirred. "I was doing good for a while," he whispered, half-awake. "Yeah you were," I said, and wiped his head.

These are the hardest times for me. That knot builds up in my throat as I try to get him comfortable again. It's the saddest, loneliest moment I've lived a hundred times before. I kissed his forehead and turned off the light, hoping he would get some rest.

March 6

Early this morning, I awoke to Stephan sobbing beside me. I rolled over and held him as he cried heavy, sad tears. I knew there was nothing I could say. I just wanted him to know he wasn't alone. Eventually, he spoke about how afraid he was—afraid of how hard it was to really confront this disease and get past it. He said he doesn't want to die yet, but he's not sure he's got the strength to get well. He's frightened that he might not succeed.

In that moment, holding him felt like such an impotent gesture. I love him deeply, and as strong as my love is, it can't prevent his pain. Still, I hug him and hope that in some way it penetrates his fears for a while.

I got a call from my brother last night asking me if I was going to his wedding next week. I never returned the RSVP. The truth is, I had forgotten about it. And suddenly, the moment of truth was here. I had to tell him about Stephan, which meant I'd have to tell the rest of my family.

I was relieved to feel Dan's support. He hoped I could make his wedding but understood if I didn't. He asked about my health and we talked for a while about little things. My next task is to tell Mom and Dad. My head hurts just thinking about it.

March 14

Stephan's progress goes up and down. He had a good weekend followed by two days of the runs. He took Lomotil and some other medicine, and now he's constipated. In spite of the confusion in his bowels, Stephan is definitely feeling better with each day. He's still low on energy, but I can see it slowly increasing. And with it comes a certain amount of frustration.

He says he sees me going out to work every day "living my life" and feels like he's left home trying to catch up.

I called Mom from work yesterday and let her know what was happening. She was speechless. I tried to keep it matter-of-fact, "We've known for about two years, but recently, it's just gotten too big to keep quiet." Mom said that she and Dad have talked about this and worried that "something like this" might happen. Before she hung up, she said she hoped to see me at the wedding Saturday, and then said, "I guess that means I hope Stephan is feeling okay."

It was the first time I ever heard her say his name or even acknowledge his existence.

March 26

I have less than two weeks left at my counseling job. Most of my cases have been transferred. I'm doing paperwork and trying to get everything in order. I've also begun training at the restaurant. It is so weird to be doing this again. In some ways, it's like riding a bicycle. In other ways, it is so foreign from what I am used to. The people I will be working with seem nice enough. Most of them are in their early '20s and like to go out after work. I suddenly feel very old.

My brother's wedding was lots of fun. In fact, I surprised myself and stayed over night so I could spend more time with my family. The truth was, it just felt good to get away from everything – the stress, the anger, the sadness. And since none of my siblings knew about Stephan's diagnosis yet, it was easy to pretend everything was okay. As usual, there were those times when I felt like a stranger within my family, watching them laugh and dance, but even that was a welcome distraction from the constant worry and disease back home.

Before the end of the weekend, I told everyone. I don't even remember what I said, I was just glad to get it out of the way. Everyone played along his or her "party lines." Those who are open and supportive offered help, those who aren't, said little. I assume there will be conversations between everyone and still, nothing will really change.

No one will visit – still. A few will call, maybe a little more frequently, but for the most part, months will roll on and they'll know nothing about Stephan and me, and our dance with death.

Stephan's health has improved slightly and seems to be holding, though it's always a guessing game for how long. Now, we're dealing with what this means in terms of our relationship. I think both of us have been so focused on surviving, we haven't noticed what is going on between us. With the realization that we have time, and Stephan's health isn't as much of a distraction, we can see what is going on more clearly.

What it boils down to is this: Stephan is alone a lot and feels useless. I'm gone most of the day working and involved in the world. He doesn't have the energy to walk to the corner, and we are limited on what we can do — and where we can do it. Still, I wanted to support him and try to keep positive.

I thought a good solution might be for him to do something creative, maybe start working on his next show. He could do it on the couch, in bed, at the kitchen table. This would give him something to do and distract him from all the daily problems he has. He liked the idea and said he'd try.

When I got home, he was already in bed, sound asleep. I miss him. I miss us.

April 16

A few friends came by for dinner last night. At first I didn't think Stephan would be able to sit at the table with us. His stomach is acting up again, and he is constantly clutching it and making these pained faces (of course he won't call the doctor). But, when it was time for dinner, Stephan was determined to at the table. It turned out to be a great evening. We laughed and talked the whole night. Stephan actually looked better as the night went on. It was so great to hear him laughing.

For a few hours, the ghost of AIDS stayed in the bedroom. It was a welcome break.

Earlier this week, we decided to go look for a pair of shoes for Stephan. We started to walk up to Market Street and I was shocked by how difficult this was for Stephan. His steps were small and he was breathing heavily. He looked like an old man. I thought, If anyone saw us walking, there is no question they'd know he was sick. Still, he moved slowly along, holding himself as erect as possible.

On our way home, he said something about being so tired and he realized how "it was probably a sign of how 'far along' he was." I hadn't thought about it in those terms. He grabbed my arm and continued walking, trying hard not to drag his feet. We had to stop and rest quite a few times before we made it to our building.

April 30

This afternoon we were lying in bed, talking and holding each other. Stephan was talking about how unattractive he felt and how he wished he could be more physical with me. The more we talked, the closer he held me and stroked my head or kissed my shoulder. And I suddenly realized what was happening… I don't remember the last time he was affectionate, even seductive with me.

I wanted so much to show him how I felt about him — about us. When I began to make advances toward him, he became rigid and tense. Everything stopped. He didn't like that I had made a move. "Everything is always so controlled for you, isn't it?" I asked, feeling hurt and frustrated. He didn't respond. I got out of bed and made an excuse about fixing dinner and went into the kitchen, angry… and horny!!

I've spent the rest of the evening trying to shake this anger. It's not easy. I bounce back and forth between being a whining martyr and an understanding best friend. Right now, the whiner is winning – I hate her.

May 20

Last night before we went to sleep, Stephan said he couldn't explain what was going on inside his head and he was trying to understand it. I asked if there was anything I could do and he looked at me and said, "Like what? You can't take away this disease. You can't give me back my energy. You can't make things any different from what they are, and you certainly can't give me back my life."

He's right. We took another walk yesterday. I just can't believe how slowly he moves now. His joints ache and he tires easily. As we were walking, he looked at me sadly and said, "I'm going to have to start using a cane soon, aren't I?" Then he covered his eyes and wiped away his tears. This proud, beautiful man who used to leap and spin across a stage was dealing with a body that betrayed him with every step.

Tonight, when I came home from work, Stephan was barely awake. We had dinner and he went right back to sleep. He woke up a little while later and called me from the bedroom. He says he's worried – he doesn't know why he's so tired or why his stomach continues to bother him (though we both know it is most likely due to lymphoma).

I asked Stephan if he thought about leaving – what it would be like. He said he just gets sad, thinking about the people he'll miss. "I won't be around to see how you or anyone else is doing ten years from now. That makes me so sad."

I started crying as he said all this. I told him I was going to miss him. Then I thanked him for all he did for me. The way he changed my life, helped me discover who I was. I said I have never been happier, or more proud of who I am and what I'm capable of – all because of what he taught me.

"I don't get it when you tell me these things," he said. I believe him. He can't see past what is in front of him right now. Doesn't matter. I know.

May 27

It feels like the summer is already half over. Time moves so quickly, leaving Stephan and me wondering if things are happening too slow or too fast. Lately Stephan has had a taste for fresh lemonade, so I've been squeezing lemons and mixing a batch every day. He takes these big gulps then sighs and closes his eyes.

When he feels up to it, we'll go to the movies or take a walk to the little lawn by Christ's Church and sit for a while. Always, the walk to and from is painfully slow. We take ten steps then wait for a minute. Stephan catches his breath, and we move on.

There seems to be little change in Stephan's health – at least, nothing dramatic. His joints still ache, his stomach remains bloated and a constant source of discomfort. Stephan spends the majority of the day in bed or in the living room with the air conditioner on. He sleeps or reads and waits for me or friends and family to come by and offer a few welcome hours of distraction.

We've established a routine, of sorts. On my days off, we spend a few hours together until he needs to rest. Then I'll either take a nap with him or I'll go into the living room and read or write. Evenings, it's the same thing. I fix dinner, spend time with Stephan, watching TV or a movie until he gets tired, usually by 9:00, then I'll go out into the living room and do the same thing again.

Tonight, my "family tape" has been playing in my head. Stephan keeps encouraging me to call my parents, to talk with them about how life is going for me. I don't know how to explain the empty feeling I get when I talk with them. Their silence weighs heavy in our conversations.

How can I share what I am feeling when they won't recognize Stephan's existence?

June 2

The past week or so has been hard for me. I came home from work on Thursday and Stephan was burning up. He had a trash can next to the bed because he thought he might get sick. There are the times when things feel so impossible, oppressive. I look at him and wonder if he'll be alive in the fall. His legs are so skinny, like a baby deer; his face has also begun to get that gaunt look.

My emotional pain has become such a regular part of my life, sitting in the background, like a constant hum. Sometimes, it swells within me and becomes so loud and I can do nothing but surrender to its sound. In tears, I moan and ride the wave. Then collapse into an exhausted sleep.

We talked yesterday about "how things were going." Stephan is feeling distant again and says he doesn't like this. Neither do I. He says I tend to isolate myself either in my writing or reading, leaving him by himself. I listened and tried not to get defensive. This is what he feels.

It is not an accusation, only a request for more time together. What I wanted to say was that he is isolating himself, too. So often, he sits, staring. I know what he thinks about: his death, his life, everything. But I know nothing about what he sees, what he feels.

In fact, he has said this to me in those exact words, "You know nothing about what I am going through." He's right. At the same time, he knows nothing about what I am going through, either. When I've tried to talk with him about this, about what I'm going through, he becomes angry and defensive. Like he is being blamed for it.

I know it is hard for him to hear what this whole experience is like for me. He can't fix it; he can't do anything about it. He is powerless, and this makes him feel guilty. So, I try not to talk to him about it because he gets so upset. He doesn't like to see me in pain – pain that he's somehow the source of.

So, we retreat into the safety of ourselves, holding onto our pain, neither wanting to look at the others. What I'm beginning to see is in this little dance, these individual battles and victories, we are learning to give each other respect and acceptance. I think what we're beginning to realize is that we can't save each other from what is happening. All we can do is be ourselves and survive.

The hardest part for me is that, as we move on, I know Stephan will be less and less available for me. Tonight I stroked his head and rubbed his back. I could feel how tired he was. Selfishly, I wished he would rub my back, too. His skin felt so soft and smooth. I tried to stifle my sobs as I rubbed him, but it got more and more difficult.

I know he heard them. When he finally fallen asleep, I went into the living room and cried even harder.

June 6

Today started off with Stephan and I talking about what's been going on. He feels more and more isolated, and said that giving up our dance company was like giving up his last reason for holding on. He cried and cried. These intense emotional moments are rare for him, and when they happen, it startles me.

Of course I needed little persuasion to cry while he spoke. I was at a loss for what to say. I know what the company meant to him. The kids were our family. He had spent years grooming them, watching them, helping them grow up. I know it is a terrible loss for him.

In the middle of our little melt down, the phone rang. It was an invitation to join some friends for brunch. I was shocked when Stephan said he wanted to go. It turned out to be a great idea. We ate and spent the day with friends we haven't seen in a long time. I kept looking at Stephan to make sure he was all right. He looked happy, so alive. It was a perfect day.

Of course now he's wiped out, in bed sleeping. He said he's going to try and stop complaining, to "be positive." I've got no expectations about this promise. He's got every right to complain. I've begun to see that when things are especially difficult, I can do little more than be who I am in that moment. I have to let go of this feeling of "should." If I am upset, I am. Period.

June 9

Stephan got sick yesterday. He woke me up because he felt uncomfortable, and within a couple of minutes, he was throwing up. All I could think was "What the fuck does THIS mean?" As it turns out, he was having a bad reaction to the synthetic morphine he had been taking. After it happened, he was shaking and kept saying, "I'm scared."

Luckily, it was over quickly and I got him back into bed where he stayed for the rest of the day. I went to work, wondering if it was a good idea to leave him alone. Fortunately, the restaurant was slow and I was home in the early afternoon. It was a humid day, the kind of day where you just want to sleep, so we did.

Today, when I got home from work, I gave Stephan a little pep talk. He played with me and tried to ignore my challenge. We talked about mentally shifting his energy and the positive effects it could have on him physically. I suggested that he was feeling sorry for himself and that he could make things different if he really wanted to.

I left to do a few chores, and when I came home, I found Stephan lying in bed, half dressed. "I tried," he said, "I really tried. I just couldn't make it." He got up and tried to get to the market two blocks away. He said he almost collapsed on the way home.

"It's getting worse, isn't it?" he asked me. "I guess it is," was all I could say. We talked again about the fact that he would be dying, soon. There were no tears this time; we simply talked in a matter-of-fact way about it. Stephan thinks he'll be dying soon, maybe before his birthday in August. I'm not so sure it'll be that soon.

He wishes he could see my first book published and be at my first reading. I wished I could always feel what I felt at that moment: love.

TAKING UP THE CROSS

The mood in our family began to change when the oldest children began to move into adolescence. Suddenly, the balance of control started shifting, they were more independent, spent more time away from the home. Once in high school, stories at the dinner table were filled with new names and places we younger kids had never heard of. There was a change in vocabulary, attitude, and style of dress. It was exciting to witness, and, like ripples in a pond, those of us only a few years younger were rocked by what was happening.

I could see my older siblings pushing against the bedrock of our parents' faith and order. There was an undertow of rebellion that rose up again and again as they grew older; skipping curfew, smoking, drinking, flunking classes. It was an endless power struggle full of slamming doors and late night shouting.

By this time, my twin, and I were inching towards our teen years, just getting ready to catch the hormonal wave that would take charge of our lives for the next few years. Any basic psych class will address the developmental need for a teenager to create a sense of self by identifying those things that make one unique, valued and different. It is THE driving theme of adolescence. Who am I? How do I fit in? What makes me important? What do I find important? And, more importantly, who shares my worldview?

As a twin, in a large family, these questions become even more difficult. How do you find what makes you unique in crowded environment that included a twin brother next to you at every turn. Self-expression wasn't easy, and could be dangerous, especially if your twin brother doesn't like it. And Tim could be very judgmental, if not mean. More than once, I felt the sting of Tim's teasing and slowly began pulling away from him as we moved closer to our teens.

So I never talked with my twin brother – or anyone else in my family for that matter – when one day, during religion class in sixth grade, I realized that none of it made any sense to me. It was one of those moments, when another part of us wakes up, takes notice, and understands that life will never be the same. I sat at my desk, staring at the chalkboard, very clear that this whole God and religion thing was all made up. It was nothing more than a big game of "Whisper Down the Lane," and here we were, thousands of years later, with a story that had been tweaked and changed countless times, and told to believe it is all true. God, sin, Jesus dying and coming back: It was a big, long, story with a happy ending that includes everyone going Heaven – as long as we were sorry for our sins and did some kind of penance.

I didn't get it. How could kneeling in front of candles and mentally rolling through a few Hail Mary's clear the slate of any black marks caused by telling a lie? And who was keeping score? Certainly God had more important things to do than watch to see if I cheated on a test or snagged a pack of gum without paying for it. My thoughts were spinning and I was trying to find a way for it to make sense.

Then came the "Aha!" moment that shook me to the core: I didn't have to believe any of it. It was both frightening and relieving. I wasn't Catholic. I didn't want to be Catholic. And… I didn't have to be a Catholic. My next thought slammed against the back of my head and almost shook me out of my seat: What do I do now?

I was 11 years old and facing a huge problem with limited choices. I already had a strong indication from watching my older siblings that resistance is not easy to express, let alone hold onto in our family. I can still see myself – feel myself – sitting in class, stuck, defeated, but very clear about what I had to do. I would have to lie.

For the next six years, I would keep my head down and play the good Catholic boy game. Once I graduated high school, I could be whoever and however I wanted. So, as a young boy just stepping into adolescence, I made a decision to keep hidden not just my true beliefs, but also the truest expression of myself, because I didn't want to create any tension or start a fight I wasn't going to win. Suddenly, my epiphany in religion created a baseline of inhibition, a self-edit mode that was constantly on.

Is it any wonder that any time my father talked with me about my grades, he would say that I wasn't "living up to my potential?" It was the absolute truth. I purposely lived an inhibited and self-conscious life.

Adding insult to inhibition, my skin was constantly breaking out in angry patches of pimples. And there was my twin brother, popular, clear-skinned, good-looking, ready-made for the spotlight.

My approach to my teen years and whatever sibling rivalry we felt was a variation on my role as family dog: I kept a low profile, stayed in the background, satisfied with the occasional pat on the head. I certainly couldn't compete with Tim. I didn't want to.

It was around this time, during a piano lesson in sixth grade, when I first decided to give up trying to keep pace with Tim. Like many things in life, we shared our Wednesday afternoon piano lessons with Sister Maria. At first, we sat on the bench together, working out those easy beginning lessons at separate ends of the keyboard. For a while, we progressed together. But Tim was a natural and took to the piano with surprising ease and pleasure. It was pretty amazing... and for me, very disheartening.

In very little time, he moved ahead of me by four, five, six lessons at a time. I struggled with learning where the keys were, practiced to get the coordination between left and right hand, and managed, at times, to show some adequate skill. But adequate pales when put next to Tim as his fingers sailed easily across the keys, his foot working the pedal like it already knew how.

One day during our piano lesson, I made an especially bad attempt at a piece and finished with my head bowed, struggling to hold back my tears. Tim, being Tim, looked at me and said, "He's crying! Look!" I quit piano shortly thereafter. I had to. There was no keeping up with my twin brother. The way he could play piano was almost eerie. Within his first year, he was playing these very difficult pieces, easily claiming the prize for best piano player in the family.

I found my thing a year later when our school started a band program. I wanted so badly to play trumpet, or saxophone, but was afraid that the rent for those instruments was too high. So I chose the cheapest instrument –

the flute – and asked my parents if I could learn to play. Like my twin brother, I showed a natural musical talent and excelled quickly in my playing.

I wish I could say I loved playing the flute, but I didn't. I loved being better at something than Tim, and I loved knowing that I had some kind of talent. But like the rest of my life, I felt stifled, unexpressed, and stuck. The fact that I was reminded over and over that the flute was a "gay" instrument, only added to my resistance.

I think that's one of the reasons I began drinking. No doubt, there was peer pressure, but it wasn't about wanting to belong as much as it was about wanting to do bad, be dangerous, and, didn't include my twin brother.

I was at an eighth grade basketball game when I had my first drinking experience. I was standing by the edge of the court, pretending to be cool and wondering if I was really pulling it off when Bill Miller came up to me and said, "I took some whiskey from my parents' bar. We're going out back to drink… wanna come?" Next to him stood Mike Mahon and James O'Toole, shrugging their shoulders and nodding. So I shrugged my shoulders with them and said, "Sure," hoping I sounded nonchalant, but secretly thrilled, scared, and especially psyched that Tim couldn't join us since he was on the basketball team.

For the next hour, we drank whiskey mixed with 7-Up and took turns sliding around on the icy parking lot behind the school. I wanted the night to go on forever. It was a social breakthrough for me. Not only had I hung out with a few of the coolest guys in our school, I had done it without my twin brother. When I told Tim about it on the way home, he looked at me and said with this annoyed, mocking voice, "What, did you get DRUNK?"

He didn't ask if I had fun. He didn't ask if he could join the next time. Instead, he found a way to dismiss my behavior with a judgmental, disqualifying tone. Still, I found a new group of friends and with it, acceptance. We weren't out of control when we drank, well, most of the time we weren't. We just loosened up and hung out, each of us learning the how and what of getting older.

There were a few occasions when I did take things too far: Once, I was plastered and broke three shelves of glasses in someone's basement bar while trying to reach for a drink. There was this incredibly loud crash that became famous amongst the eighth grade graduation stories. Then, there was the drunken three-mile bike ride home after pizza and beer at James O'Toole's house. I was literally blind drunk and finished the ride quite proud of myself for not falling, though I did end up vomiting all over my parents' bathroom.

It was one of the few times I got caught. My drinking back then was limited to once or twice a month, when we shared a bottle of Boone's Farm Strawberry Hill between four or more of us. I think Bill Miller's brother was our buyer. I had found my hook: Drinking was my way into a cooler group. It was also something that could be mine, and I loved the badness of it. Tim didn't like to drink and would typically ignore me at parties when I did.

As we moved towards the end of our grade school years, two other events set the stage for our adolescence. First was Saint David's Catholic Elementary School's production of The Living Stations.

It started in early spring of Eight grade, when Tim and I were asked to meet with Sister Carmella during lunch recess. I forgot about it and showed up late. By the time I got to Sister Carmella's classroom, Tim was already there, looking pleased with himself. Sister told me the school would be staging a live reenactment of the Stations of the Cross (Jesus' conviction and crucifixion), and that we would be the only Eighth grade students in the production — as if this would somehow make us feel special.

Tim, who had already auditioned, was given the role of the "Voice of Jesus." He would narrate the events as they unfolded, hidden behind a lectern at the front of the church. I, having shown up late, was told I would play Jesus. My job was to carry a cross around the church, stopping at different points to reenact the 14 Stations of the Cross. The Seventh grade would make up the rest of the cast: Pontius Pilate, Mary, the soldiers, Mary Magdalene, and so forth.

It was one of those moments in my life where I felt angry and cornered without options. Although I really wanted to say no, I couldn't. Doing so would open a can of worms around my beliefs and my doubts about the

Catholic religion, and that would inspire countless conversations with my parents and priests, and who knows what other consequences? Besides, saying no would break my mother's heart. What Irish Catholic mother doesn't want to see her child portray Jesus? At least, that's how I saw it. So I reluctantly stayed with my plan and played along, burying any feelings of anger or embarrassment.

No wonder alcohol became a lifeline for me. We rehearsed for two months. Mom made the robes I would wear, complete with Velcro, so that when my robes were torn, there would be a loud, realistic tearing sound! I wore a crown of thorns woven out of some willow branches, and thus endured every embarrassment imaginable for a 13-year old boy, including standing in almost naked in front of my whole school, and parish.

After our first weekend of performances, Mom showed me a letter from one of the nuns in the parish, about how wonderful I was portraying Jesus, how powerful the whole production was, and how proud she must be of her children. I finished reading it and looked at her tears in her eyes and thought, "She wants me to hug her and show her how much this means to me," and all I want to do is tear up the letter and scream about how much I hated what I was doing.

I bit my tongue and I hugged her and walked away wondering if I'd be able to make it through high school without really losing control.

The other story from Eighth grade concerns the infamous Break-In 0f '75.

In this story, Mike Mahon, James O'Toole, and Mark Doyle are Tim and my accomplices. Together, we were the 4 x 100 Eighth grade relay team. One early Saturday morning, we met to practice our passes, getting ready for the Penn Relays. Not far from our home, there was a pair of very old houses that sat off the road, partially hidden by overgrown birch trees and shrubs. One of the houses was not only empty, but missing the back wall completely. From the road, you could see through the windows to the woods behind. It looked like a set of a play, a very scary play where ghosts or other demons are hiding in the dark, looking for you.

Any time we walked past this house on our way into town, we'd talk about how it was haunted. We'd dare each other to step up to the windows and look in. But we'd always chicken out and run away before getting too close, thinking that we had heard chains clanking or a voice shouting at us.

The second house was still occupied by one of the oldest women in our parish. She lived by herself and spent her time saying the rosary in the kitchen by an old wood stove. Somewhere in our family's collection of old newspaper clippings, there is a photo of me, age 12, with Sister Maria and some of my classmates sitting in this woman's home. I am playing the piano, and we are singing a religious song as part of charitable work with the school.

After practicing baton passes with my teammates for a while on that sunny spring Saturday morning, I thought it would be fun to go take s look inside the haunted house since it was only a 10-minute walk from the track. Once we got to the house, I led the group around to the back of the house, where we found a thick layer of dead leaves covering the ground floor in what was probably the kitchen. We could make out the remains of a fire, complete with beer bottles and a bunch of crushed cigarette butts in one corner.

It took a minute for our eyes to adjust, as we moved towards the back of the exposed first floor, but way back in the far corner I saw the faintest outline of a stairwell. There was a bit of jockeying, as we all volunteered someone else to go first. Since this was my idea, I was pushed up front to take the lead. It was like something right out of The Blair Witch Project: creepy and getting creepier with each step that took us deeper into the darkness.

Barely able to see, our hands flailing out in front of me, I reached for the wall by the steps, everyone else following in shuffled steps and low voices. Once I started up the stairwell, whatever light we had was lost until we got to the top of the steps, where a lighter shade of gray suddenly seemed heavenly.

We started climbing the steps, me in front, with Mike, James, Mark, and Tim in that order behind me. Mark Doyle was muttering and sobbing about wanting to leave, but we hushed him and continued to feel our way up the steps, pushing cobwebs out of the way and trying not to fall.

I made it to the top, turned the corner of the stairwell, stepped into the room, and quickly fell to the floor screaming in fright. I couldn't believe what I was looking at! Mike was half a second behind me and did the same thing.

There in the opposite corner of the room was a body hanging from a noose.

The light was better on this floor once you turned the corner, thanks to a window on the far wall. But it still took a few seconds that it took to really understand what we were looking at. Mike and I screamed again — this time with laughter. We called the others up and roared when each of them got up the nerve to finally enter the room and look at whatever it was that was causing so much screaming.

What we thought was a body hanging from the noose was actually a mannequin. The five of us were laughing and hyperventilating on the floor for the next 10 minutes. It was one of the most frightening experiences of my life.

At some point I said, "You want to see if we can sneak a bottle of wine out of the house next door?" I heard the old woman being prayed for at Mass, and remembered my mother saying she was been in the hospital with pneumonia for a week.

I don't remember hearing a lot of resistance from anyone, so I led the group down the stairs. We snuck through the back yards, pried open a kitchen window, and all started climbing into another dark room, this one filled with furniture and old smells. Not being very skilled criminals, we stood around wondering what to do next. I began walking around the kitchen, looking at all the different bottles, but everyone else stood in place. The adrenaline rush of a few minutes ago smoldered out in this sad space.

Someone said, "I don't think this was a good idea," and we all decided to leave. I stepped onto the window ledge and began to climb out when I heard, "Hold it right there!" I look up and three policemen are pointing their guns at me, "Now, come down very slowly." Behind me, Mark Doyle, starts crying again.

We were taken to the police station where they did some kind of intake but didn't arrest or fingerprint us. We sat in a cell and stared at the floor listening to Mark Doyle worry about what his parents would do to him...and worry even more if he just ruined his chances to get into college.

For the third time that day, his freckled face turned red, and he began to cry.

For the record, our relay team did not do well at the Penn Relays a few weeks later. But, but we did take first place in the grade school championships later that spring. There was surprisingly little fallout from the Break In. Tim and I had a "talk" with our parents, and were grounded for two weeks, that was it.

I was surprised at how easy my parents were about it. When we were older, we asked why they had been so lenient, and Dad said, "We thought your experience with the police was probably enough. You didn't need more than that."

And he was right. My parents, for all their strict morals and blind faith, could show incredible insight when it came to raising their children. I walked away from "the Break In" very clear about my limits. I may have liked to drink and get a little crazy, but I wasn't interested in anything more "bad" than that — at least until I discovered pot in high school.

I know Mike and James were both grounded for a month. Mark Doyle was grounded through the summer, though I think he got into college without too much trouble.

I was entering high school a few months later, an insecure and repressed young boy waiting for the day when I could express myself freely and honestly. The fact that my twin brother was going through the same thing was not only lost on me, it didn't matter. He had the good skin, the outgoing personality, and an enviable talent. I was the smart, pimple-faced one carrying a different cross now — an endless game of charades, hoping beyond hope not to get caught.

It wasn't until many years later, when Tim and I were in our thirties; grown and comfortable in who we were as adults that I was able to take comfort in one of the most important facts about being a twin – it never ends.

AIDS Timeline #4

January 8, 1988, the World Health Organization states that AIDS cases worldwide have increased by 56%.

October 6, 1988, the Department of Justice states that people living with AIDS/HIV can no longer be discriminated against.

October 11, 1988, a major demonstration is organized by ACT UP outside the FDA to protest the lack of action regarding drug development for AIDS. 80 people are arrested.

By the end of 1988, HIV/AIDS has become the third leading cause of death among men 25-44. One year later, it is the second leading cause, surpassing heart disease, cancer, suicide, and homicide.

April, 1989, the Immigration Department detains HIV+ visitor Hans Verhof while he is attempting to attend a conference in San Francisco.

September 14, 1989, ACT UP stages a demonstration at the New York Stock Exchange protesting the price of AZT. Burroughs eventually lowers the drug price 20%.

June 15

I signed up for a writing workshop; it begins at the end of the month. When I told Stephan, he surprised me and started crying. He said he was proud of me for following through on my goals. He was crying because he'd never be able to see what becomes of my writing. Then he asked again why I stayed around and why I didn't complain. I don't answer these questions anymore; I've decided it's not necessary. I held him close to me and cried along with him.

I guess in a strange way, I have become an inspiration to Stephan. The past few days when I came home, he's had stories about what he has done. He took a trip to the market and bought flowers and arranged them in a vase in the living room. He walked to Christ's Church and watched the children play. These are small things that have become major victories in the constantly shrinking world that has become his life.

Today, when I got home, Stephan was sleeping on the sofa; the air conditioning was whirring away. There were boxes and bags lying all around him. When I kissed him, he woke up and smiled at me, "I had the most wonderful day."

He walked up to South Street and bought a pair of sandals he has been wanting for more than a year; they cost more than $200. Then he decided to check out a sale at the Gap, where he spent another $200 on shorts and shirts. When he got home, he put on his favorite Motown tape and tried all the different clothes on and danced around the living room. In my mind, I could see him putting on Martha and the Vandelles, swinging his hips back and forth in his new shorts, feeling as if he were twenty-five and healthy.

Hearing him tell that story, seeing that little smile behind his eyes, it's the best thing that's happened around here in a long time.

June 16

I spoke to Mom today, since she was out of town on her birthday. She thanked me for the card — I hadn't sent one. I assume one of my sisters signed my name for me. Then she said she was sorry I missed my birthday dinner — they had it without me. That was more than a month ago! I honestly don't remember what happened and why I didn't go. I think I couldn't get someone to stay with Stephan, or else I just didn't feel up to it. Either way, I felt immediately sad.

I really don't miss my family when I don't see them. Eventually, I know they'll call, or I will. I know they haven't got a clue about what to do, especially Mom and Dad. And that makes me sad. They can't listen to their hearts and comfort their son who is scared and tired. I can't imagine what it must feel like to be a parent who is bound to their child and their faith.

They don't ask how he is. With the slightest hesitation, Mom will ask how I am, looking for deeper meanings behind my one word answers. I keep it vague and just say it's been a rough week, but things seem to be improving a little.

This seems to satisfy her, and explains why I didn't make it to my birthday dinner. I don't think I even called to say I wouldn't make it. Neither of us has found any steady ground to work from when it comes to Stephan. I offer these timid comments emphasizing what WE are doing, or I'll say Stephan's name in passing. There is this measured tone to her responses, a cautious search for middle ground.

I get confused and infuriated by the way their morals immobilize them, and me. And to remain firm in that faith — I don't think I'll ever know that kind of faith. I'm not sure I want to.

July 1

Since I signed up for my writing workshop, I decided it would be a good idea to have a story to work with. I finished my first draft last night. I know it needs a work, but I am excited about what I have done. I read it to Stephan and he liked it, too.

Tonight we went out to dinner to celebrate. Stephan wasn't feeling very good, but he wanted to go out, so we did. He got dressed in the new clothes he bought; it was very cute. The restaurant was only a block away, and it didn't require much effort to get there.

We had a date! We kept the conversation light, held hands across the table, and sipped wine. There was a little of what it used to be like – for a while – and I drank it all in.

Stephan went straight to bed when we got home, he was pretty beat. I sat on the couch smoking a cigarette, and, not for the first time, wondered about what my next relationship will be like. What stories will I tell over dinner? One time, not too long after getting together, Stephan and I spent a night drinking wine and playing songs from our favorite albums—lights off, candles lit. It's one of many favorite memories that come up when I'm walking. And now I wonder, what music will my new man play? Which songs will become ours?

Yesterday I read an article in the gay paper about an AIDS related infection, MAC that has been the subject of research over the past year. I think this is what Stephan has. At least, the symptoms are the same. I'm hoping Stephan won't see it.

According to the article, patients who began to display the symptoms (fatigue, night sweats, abdominal pain...) all died within four to six months.

This didn't mean anything. That's all I kept telling myself after I read it. Then, I was saying those same words to Stephan when he was shaking the article in my face. "This is me. Did you read this? Everything in here describes me." I thought I threw the paper out.

Last night, I found Stephan crying in bed. He couldn't stop. His symptoms not only had a name, but a time limit. MAC made it real for Stephan, and he was scared. I was, too.

July 6

Stephan is scheduled for another bronchoscopy tomorrow. He says he's been feeling like something's wrong and spoke to his doctor, and here we go again. At first I was taking it in stride. After all, we've been through this several times. Then it occurred to me this evening that if it is positive for pneumonia, he might not be strong enough to take a month of treatments.

Since he read that article, he's accepted something, and within days, he's grown remarkably weaker. It's an effort for him to get out of bed. His arms tremble as he leans on them, and I often have to help him sit up.

Tonight he was in bed when I came home, and he felt a little feverish. "What'll we do if it is positive?" he asked. I didn't answer; I didn't have one for him. He knows what he's up against. He kept saying he was too tired to be scared, but he asked me to stay with him until he fell asleep.

July 8

The procedure was not as easy for Stephan this time around. I think they used less anesthesia since he was so weak. Whatever it was, he threw up twice and was awake the whole time. He was not looking too hot when I found him in the recovery room.

Stephan's doctor called about an hour after we had gotten home. Stephan was right: They found pneumonia. I immediately burst into tears. Stephan said he was too exhausted to cry; he just lay in bed staring. The next step is a short outpatient procedure to get a catheter inserted so they can begin medication. He's getting ten days of it. The doctor doesn't believe Stephan could handle more. I think he's right.

In my spare moments, I have started to imagine living in other cities, moving on, life after Stephan has gone. I can't help it. There's a curious combination of excitement and sadness. I can't decide if these little mind trips are a way of creating my future, or am I just running away from everything that has happened here?

July 9

After working until 1:30 this morning, I got up at 5:00 so that Stephan could be at the hospital by 6:00. The procedure to get the catheter turned out to be fairly simple. Stephan's first treatment was this afternoon. The doctor is now pushing for fourteen treatments, so we've got thirteen to go.

July 11

For now, Stephan is doing fine. The catheter isn't bothering him too much, and if it does, he has a painkiller to help. I'm just trying to get through. I know the side effects will begin soon, and he'll be getting more irritable.

I told Stephan this morning that he was like a '67 Chevy. He keeps on needing some engine work, but he never dies. We both got a laugh out of that and then started doing the Monty Python skit, "Bring out your dead." This made us laugh even harder. Stephan kept grabbing at his chest where the catheter was, saying "Oh! Oh! Don't make me laugh!"

July 12

When I got home, I started talking with Stephan about how hard it is for me this time, and within seconds I started crying—harder than I can remember ever crying before. Stephan stroked my head and patted my back, listening quietly. I felt terrible to be dumping this on him, and he said he was glad that I did. He thought I was taking things too much in stride.

Stephan has become very calm – accepting – about being sick again. He said this was the fourth time; he wasn't going to put any energy into worrying or trying to get better. That became too tiring before. So he's adopted this steady pace and moves through his day as best he can. Makes sense to me. I'm not sure I have the same ability.

July 14

Stephan has finished his sixth treatment. It's getting pretty hard for him. Today he seemed to get a little disoriented, kind of drunk, while we ate lunch. He moved slowly and his eyes stayed at half-mast.

I helped him into bed and he fell asleep before I even pulled the sheet over him. Now, his doctor is questioning if he'll be able to handle fourteen days of treatment. No kidding. Tomorrow they will run blood tests, and we'll see how the treatments are going.

July 16

To my surprise, even with all the activity around Stephan's treatments, I have finished rewriting my story for my writing group. This group has become one of the most positive things I could have done. It keeps me focused on something unaffected by Stephan's health. It is an odd group of people, though, especially the guy hosting it. He likes to write love poems to his wife and then read them while drinking sherry and toasting her. Still, there are others in the group who offer good feedback. At minimum, it's an evening out where no one knows about Stephan or anything about that part of my life.

Stephan was pretty sad this morning. He was staring out at nothing and I asked what was wrong. "I can't do anything I used to. I just want that back," he said, tears falling as he bit his lip. "Even street people are better off than me. They can make some choices. I don't have any freedom. And I just want to be normal again." I'm not afraid to die. I just don't feel like I'm ready – at least not mentally."

He had to get ready to see his doctor, so he shuffled around the apartment getting dressed, combing his hair. I wonder what it feels like to have your life drip away from you until suddenly, you're feeling less than half empty. But your mind? Your mind hasn't gotten there yet.

Stephan was breathing heavily before we even got to the elevator at the end of the hall. "I just want to die," he said hoarsely as we walked. I'm wondering when Stephan's mind will accept what is happening.

He seems to be getting closer, and I think this confuses (and maybe startles) him.

July 18

After his doctor appointment yesterday, Stephan sat down and said, "I've made a decision. I'm going to try my best to get through the full fourteen days of treatment. Chances are, the pneumonia will come back again. When it does, I'm not going through this treatment again. It doesn't make any sense to." His voice was low and steady; his words seemed carefully thought out. "I just want to give this one last good fight. That way, when it comes time, no one can say I didn't try." With these words, he lifted his chin a little and took a deep breath. He can be pretty amazing... still.

He asked me to help him get ready to die. If we were lucky, he had another four to six months. He didn't know what to do, how to prepare. I don't know that I'm much of an expert, either, but I said I'd help.

I didn't feel sad as he talked. I listened to his words and sat with him. He is such a proud man, but he's also practical. I know he wants everything to end soon. He sees how hard it is getting on me and everyone else around him.

For now, I'm interested in getting through these treatments. He's getting weaker and weaker. Now, he has trouble standing to take a shower or even to brush his teeth. We move around the apartment arm in arm, his weight on me. Last night, he talked about getting a cane to help him walk. Then he said he'd never let himself be seen in public with it.

July 20

With four days left of treatment, Stephan is wiped out. That drunken stupor that usually passes after he naps stays with him all the time. Still, yesterday we had a whole slew of visitors come throughout the day. Stephan talked and listened, pushing himself to stay awake. I think we were both relieved to have other people around to distract us. It's been intense.

This morning we were supposed to go to the hospital so that Stephan could get a transfusion. It was rescheduled for Wednesday. I'm glad. I wasn't up for hanging around the hospital for four hours while Stephan got transfused. I doubt I'll feel any more positive about it by Wednesday, but for today, it's one less thing to consider.

Once again, I find myself looking at the financial rut we are stuck in. I haven't been making very good money at the restaurant; in fact, last week, I only made $250. Half of July's bills aren't paid yet; and August is less than two weeks away. I'm looking for another part-time position that can bring in better money. There's a bartending position available at The Black Banana, an after hours, gay club right down the street. I'm going to apply.

July 22

We were at the hospital by 7:00 today for Stephan's transfusion. We already know what to expect from this, we've gone through it before. If it will help for a little while, I guess it's worth it.

Stephan says he still feels like the pneumonia is back. We met with his doctor, who said Stephan's lungs looked pretty clear. He suggested that what Stephan is feeling could be any number of things: the side effects from the treatment, side effects from the virus, or just the result from "any number of smaller infections attacking Stephan's body."

Some comfort.

Today was particularly hard for me. I made less than $50 at work (again), and when I came home, Stephan was sitting up in bed, moving in slow motion, trying to dry off. I got him a towel and heard the words "This is getting too hard" play over and over in my head. I fought my tears, got Stephan settled, and walked out into the living room where the words sounded even louder, echoing over and over in my head. "This is getting too hard." Each time I heard the phrase, a new surge of tears welled up from the pit of my stomach. I grabbed a pillow and pushed my face in it to stifle my sobs so that I didn't disturb Stephan.

FAITH TRUMPS FAMILY

Like most gay men and women, I always had a sense of being different from everyone else as a child. I was definitely more sensitive and less athletic than the other boys in the family, which didn't necessarily make me gay, but it certainly colored others perception of me. By the time I was nine or ten, I had secret man crushes on a few different TV stars: Bill Bixby in "The Courtship of Eddie's Father," the two guys from "The Mod Squad," Mr. Dixon from "Room 222." And of course, there was "Emergency!" with two of the sexiest guys ever on TV – Randolph Mantooth (my favorite) and Kevin Tighe.

I couldn't wait for these shows to come on, and would stare at these men in wonder. Instinctively, I knew I had to keep these crushes secret. I couldn't tell you why, but I knew.

A few years later, I had my first gay "aha" moment. I was walking back through the woods behind our house with one of my older brothers. We made our way to "The Rocks," a small hilltop dominated by three huge boulders overlooking the creek. On the backside of the hill, we found the remains of a fire, several empty beer cans, some scattered cigarette butts, and a Playboy magazine. The public school kids had been here the night before.

My brother quickly grabbed the Playboy and the two of us started looking at page after page of naked women. My first thought was, how could someone be so openly sexual, so naked! To be that shameless was completely foreign to me. I was excited, and horrified at the same time. My next thought was, "What's the big deal? Why do guys make so much noise about breasts?"

I didn't wonder what these woman felt like, had no desire to hold them. I didn't understand the attraction, at all. As for vaginas, I stared at each photo in frightened disbelief. What were we supposed to do with that?!

I didn't necessarily equate this experience with being gay – at that time I didn't really know what that word really meant – except that's what the feminine boys (including me) were called. That there was a life and lifestyle behind the word were completely lost on me.

What I knew was what I saw around me. The path was set: guys dated girls; they went to college, met their wife, got married and had kids. This was my world. I may have felt "different," but at that age, I didn't know I had another choice. I didn't know I had any choice.

Still, as I sat next to my brother paging through that magazine, I knew enough to pretend I liked what I was looking at, and to keep secret the questions I had about my sexuality.

Truth be told, since sex was never talked about in our house, it wasn't hard to keep a secret. My parents, who never shared anything more than a chaste kiss in front of their children, had some secrets of their own. Each night, as if to announce their sexual innocence, they kept their bedroom door open. Mom always claimed it was so she could hear, if one of us should need her.

But even after the children had grown past the need for a late night hug after a bad dream, the bedroom door sat open, denying my parents – and their children – any sense of intimacy.

The only time Dad tried to talk with Tim and me about sex was a complete disaster. One night after dinner, he asked us to join him for a quick trip into town. Once in the car, and on our way, Dad shut the radio off and said, "At your age (we were 13), you might start to notice hair growing under your arms... and down there." His hand moved off the steering wheel and hesitantly circled above his crotch.

I sat in the back seat stunned. I couldn't believe what I was hearing. Thankfully, Tim was there in the passenger seat to take care of the conversation. First, he clicked his tongue, then he let out a big sigh. "This is important, Tim! I need you to pay attention." Dad said impatiently. Tim, with equal impatience, responded, "Yeah, we know Dad. We read about this stuff in a book Joe Donahue's parents gave him – a year ago!"

It was true. The summer after sixth grade, when his parents were out, our best friend Joe Donahue showed Tim and me a book about sex his parents had given him for his birthday. We each took a turn with the book up in the attic so we could read it in privacy. It's curious, to look back and see that even in the most innocent, instructional context, we chose to explore and learn about sex privately.

I will never forget sitting in that stifling attic, looking at these cartoon drawings of men and women over and over. The female anatomy was foreign and uninteresting to me. But the male? I was much more interested in what was happening on that side of the page. I kept reading this section over and over, trying to stifle an erection as I looked at the anatomical drawings of a man's genitals. It was another moment when I knew my questions and feelings had to be stifled. I joined the other two and pretended I couldn't wait to have sex with a girl.

Back in the car, I felt bad for Dad. I could see the disappointment in his eyes. This was supposed to be one of those father/son moments. He stared ahead, completely at a loss. "Well… do you have any questions?"

True to form, Tim closed the conversation with a resounding, "No!" Which wasn't completely true. We just didn't have any questions for him. The rest of the ride to and from town was filled with electrified shame, and guilt.

I didn't see Joe Donahue's sex book before my first ejaculation, so I had no idea what was happening when it happened. It was frightening. I really thought something was wrong with me, but there was no way I could tell anyone what I had done to make puss come out of my penis.

I thought I was some kind of medical freak… had nightmares about going to specialists. I was afraid I would be put in an institution – but it felt so good I could stop doing it. When I realized after a few days that nothing bad was happening – or would happen – I became a champion masturbator! Five, six, even seven times a day. And every time, I found that sweet, intense, powerful release! Mom clearly saw the results of my efforts in the laundry. Being the eighth boy, I'm sure I wasn't the first. Who knows WHAT she had to say about it or how many rosaries she prayed for the lust in her boys.

When I was twelve years old, I had my first kiss was in the basement of a friend's house with my girlfriend Bernadette. We had been dating for two weeks (which basically meant writing notes to each other during geography class and holding hands at recess). While Elton John's "Crocodile Rock" played on the stereo, we snuck into a corner. It was everything a first kiss should be; awkward, uncomfortable, and felt like it lasted for ten minutes. It ended abruptly, when Bernadette pushed me away and laughed, "You kiss like a vacuum!" We broke up shortly after that.

My dating didn't improve much over the next few years, though not for lack of trying. And my attempts were quite sincere. I wanted to date girls. I believed I liked girls. It's what I saw around me, and I wanted to fit in. I convinced myself I could have a future with a wife and kids. So what if I liked to make frequent trips to the locker room at the swim club, hoping to see a few men naked. I rationalized that this was my way of understanding how to be a man.

Still, I would stare every time Shirley's boyfriend, Carmine, showed up onscreen during "Laverne and Shirley!"

For me, adolescence became this huge emotional seesaw, filled with anxiety, fear, hope, desire. Inhibited, self-conscious, and no one to talk to, my mind was in constant motion. I was always on guard, squelching fear, watching what I said – and how I said it. Maybe I was… Maybe I wasn't gay. Maybe I was just a fem-boy trying to understand what it meant to be masculine… maybe if I tell someone, they can help me… I want to have a family… I want to kiss that boy… someone's going to beat me up one day… is there anyone else like me… why is this so hard…

When I met my girlfriend sophomore year, I was saved from all of that adolescent angst. Maria was my first real love – well, as real as love gets when you're in high school. I'm not exaggerating when I say this relationship saved me. I was the ugly duckling, the one who liked to stay in the background. I was scared to death of anything associated with dating or sexuality. My skin was a mess, and… I kissed like a vacuum. In spite of all this, Maria liked me, and wanted to spend time with me. It was a huge boost of confidence – especially since my twin brother didn't have a girlfriend.

Not only did Maria teach me how to kiss, but dating her also gave me what I will call "Straight Cred." For three years, I was the Drum Major and played flute in the band (could I have been more of a walking gay cliché?). Having a girlfriend who was beautiful and popular reduced the chances of getting picked on and fed the denial I held onto about my own sexuality. How could I be gay, if I got aroused when I was fooling around with Maria in the back of the family van after a date? Never mind the emotional rush I had to squelch every time I was in the gym locker room. After all, I had a girlfriend, I couldn't be gay.

Looking back now, I can see why I got drunk so often on weekends. I was miserable. Back then I thought I was having a good time. I was the life of the party – and everyone told me so on Monday mornings sitting around the cafeteria table before class. Truth be told, I was a frightened, confused, misunderstood young man. It's a tribute to Halls Cough Drops (to hide my liquor-breath) and some amazing self-control that I didn't get caught more often.

There was one high school dance, though, when too much Jim Beam landed me in the disciplinarian's office, where I have this vague recollection of sneering drunkenly at Father Boyle, and saying, "Wanna… hear my connn… fession father?" He looked at me in all seriousness and said, "If you think it will help."

I don't really remember what I said after that, but I have this fuzzy, flash of memory where I am saying the word masturbation, which may have led to a conversation where I say something about being gay. I'm not sure. What I do remember is being half-carried out to a car a little later, shouting back to Father Boyle, "Thanks for the confession!" then laughing hysterically to myself.

When I saw him at school the next Monday (still feeling hung over), Father Boyle nodded at me in the hallway, and walked past me without a word.

Against the background of all this sexual turbulence, there was a larger drama playing out in my family. In spite of – or maybe, because of – our parents' chaste example, sex and sexuality managed to rear their ugly heads at home. First, there was our oldest sister, Rosemary, a fiery beauty who was in a constant power struggle with our parents. She got engaged while still in high school to a football player from the public school. Since Rosemary wouldn't turn 18 until the December after high school graduation, she was still under my parents care, and they were very clear – she couldn't marry this guy, and she was forbidden to see him.

More than once, we were ushered out of the house, as talks became arguments that grew louder and louder. I remember once hearing Rosemary scream at the top of her lungs, "I don't want to meet with any god-damned priest." It was a tense, frightening time in our family that came to a screeching halt two days after Rosemary turned 18, when she announced to the family that she was moving out.

A week later, during dinner, our parents told us that Rosemary had been married earlier that day. None of us had been told about it ahead of time. None of us knew anything about it until that moment. I couldn't believe what was happening. Mom was saying something about loving Rosemary, but not supporting the marriage, but I wasn't listening.

I kept thinking, "How could my parents do something like this?" I was furious that we had been kept in the dark about something so important, and remember storming out of the kitchen shouting, "Why would you do this to Rosemary? I thought we were a family! Why weren't we included in any discussion about this? Why didn't you talk to us about it?"

It was the day our family was torn apart. And for me, the line was clearly drawn: My parents and their Catholic faith on one side, and I was on the other. I had three more years at home, and the message from my parents was loud and clear: Faith Trumps Family.

A few weeks later, we learned the real reason why none of us had been in attendance at the wedding: Rosemary was pregnant.

About a year after Rosemary got married, Dad sat Tim and I down to let us know that our oldest brother, Matt, was living with his girlfriend. He and Mom had suspected for a while, and apparently Dad made a surprise visit to Bloomsburg College, where Matt was now working. Dad looked at us with a very serious face and said they were sharing the same bed. We both looked at Dad and said, "So?" He was shocked at our ambivalence and began lecturing us about morals and faith and what was right.

I couldn't take it anymore. It was time to draw a line of my own. I looked directly at Dad and said, "What makes you think your morals are mine!" He pulled back blinking, as if I had taken a swing at him. "I don't agree with what the church says," I continued. "I don't think it's a big deal, what Matt's doing."

Not that it mattered. The fallout was no surprise. Matt's girlfriend was not welcome in the house as long as she and my brother continued their "immoral lifestyle." I remember more than once reading letters Matt wrote to the family where large portions were blacked out in thick marker – the paragraphs where he mentioned girlfriend's name, were censored. My parents were not backing down.

Faith Trumps Family, even in the mail.

It was another one of those moments where I felt incredibly angry and frustrated, but knew there was little I could say or do to make the situation different. And for the first time, I worried about what this meant for me. I held tighter to whatever questions I had about my sexual identity, more afraid than ever of how my parents would react to them. I just had to get to graduation.

And what about graduation? and my future? What can an insecure, unexpressed, young man with no sense of self say, when asked what his plans were after high school? My favorite classes were English and Psychology, and like the guy from the movie, "Almost Famous," I dreamed of writing for Rolling Stone magazine. I poured over every issue, read certain articles and interviews over and over. I used to imagine myself doing in-depth undercover stories about drugs or teen-age drinking, or interviewing of Billy Joel. I liked the idea of traveling to different places, exploring cultures and people and writing stories about those experiences.

When I mentioned my writing idea to Dad, he said, "I don't know what kind of living people can make as a writer. It would be a good idea to choose some other field too, just in case. A little something to fall back on." When I expressed interest in studying abroad, he again played the fiscal card and worried how I could afford it. He said it was good to have dreams, but it was also important to be practical on where I set my sights.

It was one of the most disappointing conversations I ever had with my father. He didn't encourage me to look for funding and grants; he didn't help me find a way to fulfill my dreams. In truth, I don't think he understood the creative/expressive part of me looking for release. He was a child of the Depression, his focus was always on more concrete things: getting food on the table and bills paid.

As expected, being an insecure, unexpressed, young man with no sense of self, I took my father's advice. I chose a more practical approach to college and my future. I would become a teacher. I told myself I could use my summers off to write. Only I never did any writing. I just surrendered to what I thought I was supposed to do, like everything else about my life at the time. It was the easiest solution.

I want to be clear, even with all the sexual angst, the feeling of repression, and all the unavoidable rebellion that pushed and pulled at our family, that tension was balanced by moments when our family got along. Whatever the disagreements we kids had with our parents, there was always a foundation of love. Love never went away.

For those of us still living at home during those "moral crises" in our family, I think the bonds between us grew stronger. We were lucky enough to have each other for support – and comic relief. We have countless stories from those years that still bring a roar of laughter whenever we are together.

But the idyllic Waltons image from our childhood had been tarnished, at least for me.

Faith Trumped Family – twice – and our world completely changed. It wasn't a bloodbath, but there was a lot of wreckage. I moved through my senior year more determined than ever to get away from the stifling umbrella of my parents and their faith. For me, the day I graduated was the day I would really start to live my life.

AIDS Timeline #5

January 17, 1990: The New York Times reports the federal government recommends reducing the dose of AZT (still the only drug approved for treatment of AIDS) by half. Studies showed that ore than half of all AIDS patients were not able to tolerate the higher dose (up to 1,200 mg daily), and suffer debilitating side effects, such as anemia, fatigue, shortness of breath, and neuropathy. Many patients required multiple transfusions in order to continue taking AZT. New studies indicated that the lower dose was just as effective in treating AIDS.

April, 1990: In Chicago, Women with ACT take over the intersection in front of Cook County Hospital with mattresses, declaring it the "Cook County Women's AIDS Unit," since no women with AIDS are allowed treatment in the hospital. The Cook County Hospital AIDS Unit admits its first women two days later.

April, 1990: 80,000 Haitians and supporters march across the Brooklyn Bridge to protest federal guidelines that exclude blood donations from Haitians because of their "perceived HIV risk."

July 27

When I came home from work last night, Stephan was sound asleep. I am more and more shocked by how childlike he appears, especially curled up under the covers. He looks so young and at peace; sleep is a temporary break from his fading life. There was the moist hint of perspiration as I kissed his forehead. He even smelled like sleep.

Soft. Sweet. He startled a little as my lips touched his head and I whispered, "It's me, baby, go back to sleep. I love you." He let out this sigh and his energy seemed to shift, relax. I pulled the sheet up to his rough chin. The room had this soft, gentle feeling. Safe. Everything is all right as I stand in the room, and I want to hold onto this completeness – even if it's just for a while.

The realities of our situation push against the quiet of this scene and I fight the insistent voices that say, "We've got no money." I take a deep breath. "This will be gone by tomorrow." I silently hush these words. "What do I do about my family?" I close my eyes and listen to Stephan's silent breathing. I was jealous of Stephan at that moment, so far away from the worries haunting my head. I left the bedroom and took my place on the sofa with my book and a cup of tea.

July 28

Stephan went back into the hospital last night. He had a fever of 105. I called his sister at midnight and we brought him up to the emergency room. There was only one doctor available, and he hadn't even seen the people who had come in three hours earlier. We were told it would be best to go home.

I didn't sleep too well. I woke up every hour, waiting to hear from the hospital. Finally, I called at 7:00 and the nursing supervisor said that Stephan was "in stable condition and resting." Nothing like a generic answer to relieve my anxiety.

I called hospital information and got the direct number to Stephan's room. He was in the E.R. until about 6:00 this morning. His temp has been staying around 103-104. The doctors say he's got an infection – they're just not sure of its source. My guess is that Stephan will be in for a few days, nothing long-term. He absolutely hates being there. I know he's pretty pissed.

Last night I dreamt that Stephan had died. I was furious. I kept yelling and yelling, first at Stephan, then at my parents.

July 31

After 3 days, there was still no clear idea of where or what the infection is. Stephan was so miserable – only miserable seems too nice a word to describe his mood. He asked his doctor to keep him on Demerol the whole time he was in the hospital. His doctor heard this and decided a psych consult was in order.

Stephan was so angry. "I don't think they get it," he said over the phone. "What am I supposed to do? Stick my chest out and act like I can get through this? I can't do that. I won't. They have no idea what its like…" He went on like this for a while. I got lost in his words, every so often hearing him say, "Get Ready." I think he was talking about the psychiatrist and how he was going to give the guy a hard time. All I kept hearing was "Get Ready." For what? And, how?

Stephan's back home now, and he brought his foul mood with him. "Why bother with any of this shit? I'm not really living anymore." He is so angry! He even got angry with me because I got up and began my day as if everything were normal. I put the coffee on, threw some clothes in the washer, put on the morning news – the whole time he sulked in bed.

When I sat in the chair next to him with my coffee, he looked at me and said, "Things are not the same anymore." Tears fell onto the pillow. "We worked so hard and still my body betrayed me. How long do you think before it starts again? It will… you know it."

He's right. Things will steadily get worse. I know that. I watch Stephan; he's like a caged animal. His heart is having a hard time believing his body. He just cried into his hands. I have to find the strength to help him – again, and again, and again...

August 2

A few friends we haven't seen in a while came down for the weekend, offering a break from the tension that's been bubbling up in the apartment. When I got home from work tonight, they were sitting on the bed, talking. Stephan looked relaxed, even happy.

I can't thank our friends enough, Stephan's family, too.

His niece has been over the past two days cooking and cleaning for us. And his sister continues her daily visits, charging into the bedroom with her unbridled energy. We've become a tag team, of sorts. When she comes in, I leave and do my best to recharge my battery. I can see all this beginning to take its toll on her, though. She looks a little haggard, and sometimes her affect seems kind of forced, her smile a little too big. It makes me wonder what I look like to other people—not that I really want to find out. I'd probably want to hide if I got a good look at myself.

Right now, Stephan is sleeping. For the first time in over a week, I was able to sit at the computer tonight and concentrate on writing. I got more work done on my story. Quite honestly, it felt good to escape into another world for a while.

August 4

I spoke with Mom and Dad for more than a half hour last night. I can honestly say this is the first time I felt like an adult in talking with them. We started off with the usual, safe stuff, then, during a lull in the conversation, I asked why they were so hesitant to talk to me about Stephan and his health. My heart was pounding in my ears, my hand was shaking as it held the phone, but my voice stayed steady.

I told them how hard things had been, how tired I felt. Dad, never being big on the emotional stuff, began the usual catch phrase coaching he does. Only this time, I heard it, and got that this was the best he could offer: practical advice about getting rest and believing in yourself. Mom's voice quivered, and she said something about wanting to give me a hug. I blinked back my tears and said I could use one.

When I got off the phone, I felt lighter than I've felt in a long time. I talked openly about my relationship, and how scared and angry I felt, and – how committed I was. There was a respect I felt from them that I had never experienced before. Not that what they had to say was original or mind-blowing. Basically, they encouraged me to be who I was, and to allow for my own feelings of weakness and pain. Dad suggested that I take some time to sit and close my eyes – rest, "even pray." Mom talked about when Granddad was sick and how she felt just before he died. She said, "I prayed for God to take him… just so I could feel better."

Naturally, before they hung up, they gave me the name of a priest they knew who was a "specialist" in dealing with AIDS. I didn't realize priests started "specializing" in different areas. There's no way I'm calling him, in fact I threw the number out after we hung up. But, I walked away from that conversation feeling more connected to my parents than I had in a long time.

August 10

Last night, Stephan woke me up around 2:30. His temp was 104. Rather than deal with the emergency room bullshit, we decided to try giving him a Percocet and hope the fever would break. Fortunately, it did.

I don't feel so fortunate today, though. When Stephan called me to this morning because he wanted water, I noticed the incision around his port looked horrible. It was open and full of puss. His fever was up again, too. I called the doctor's office, and we got an appointment for 3:00 this afternoon.

We sat in his doctor's office and heard exactly what I expected. Stephan was being admitted. I looked over at him, and he stared straight ahead, saying over and over in a shaky voice, "I'm not going to get upset about this."

It's now 8:30 P.M. I've just gotten home from the hospital. I cried and sobbed before I left him, then took my time walking back to our apartment. Treatment will start tomorrow; tonight he's getting another port of some kind put in on the other side of his chest. They're also doing a colonoscopy tomorrow. I don't know exactly what they're looking for. I guess it's just a precautionary.

Now I have our place to myself again. I've armed myself with videos for distraction and the answering machine to screen phone calls. It's hard to know how to feel about everything. We've been at this place more than once. He could come home and be fine, or he could get worse. There's not anticipating which way the coin lands.

Stephan is quiet, stuck inside his head and I don't have any real sense of what he feels. All I can do is wait, and watch videos. As it got close to midnight, I realized I hadn't had anything to eat since lunch. I went next door to Old City Pizza. It was almost closing time, and there was no one else there. All they could offer was the pizza leftover from the night. I ordered a small with green pepper and onion.

I bought a pack of cigarettes and sat in the middle of the restaurant, smoking and waiting while the clean up continued around me. I just stared at myself in the window's reflection. If I squinted, I couldn't recognize who I was looking at. I was a different person, just a guy having a cigarette, waiting for his pizza. That was kind of nice.

August 11

I slept horribly last night. It was humid and I felt very restless. It wasn't until after 2:00 I finally turned out the light and turned off the TV. What's to say about today? It was long and boring and rainy. I went to the gym for a half-hearted workout (which is better than none, I guess) and took a cab to the hospital.

It was pouring and thundering by the time I walked into Stephan's room. He looked like he usually does when he's in the hospital; gaunt. He was still high from the Demerol used during the colonoscopy, and he whispered that he was checking himself out in two days. "I went back on my word by coming in the hospital," he said. I understood Stephan's wish to be home, but the truth is that I don't want him there. Not if he's going to keep on getting sicker and sicker.

I feel like a robot when he's home. I just get him what he needs and try to keep our lives as together as possible. It is draining and it hurts.

Then there is his family. As wonderful and loving as they are, it's hard to find a moment of quiet and relax when they visit. I feel trapped, on guard, and a need to be polite when I just want to hang out in my underwear and not see anyone.

The worst part about this whole fucked up situation is that I know it won't be over for quite a while. I can see it... Stephan's still got some strength left.

August 14

It was a hard day for me. I felt depressed and sluggish all day. I set the alarm early to go work out but didn't feel like getting out of bed, which only made me feel guilty for not going, which made me feel angry for feeling guilty.

My whole world is not my own. Stephan comes home tomorrow, and with him comes the responsibility of taking care of him and losing any private time to him and his family. All the while people are telling me to take care of myself. Somehow that doesn't seem possible.

Today, I made it through a slow day at work, after forgetting my shoes and having to run back home to get them. It was difficult to be there today. I didn't want to banter with the people I work with; I didn't want to play nice to my customers. They all annoyed me. Everyone seemed happy and I just felt out of place.

On my way to work, there was a couple walking behind me and the woman was laughing and having a good time. I couldn't stand it. Her voice was like nails scraping a chalkboard.

August 16

Mom called the other day to invite me to dinner. I haven't been up to see Mom and Dad since Christmas. It was a great visit. No one asked about Stephan, and I didn't offer. We were all just looking for a chance to enjoy each other's company for a while. I know I was. So for a few hours, my life with Stephan was (thankfully) suspended. I stayed longer than I expected. It was a comfortable, effortless visit. I don't remember the last time I felt this good leaving their house.

August 18

Stephan came home and we are back in the same old, same old. His temp has gone up a little again. Who knows what it's from? The wound from where the incision was made from the port still hasn't healed completely. Every day, twice a day, I change the dressing and put more antibiotic cream on it. I can't tell if it's getting any better or not.

Whatever is wrong with Stephan, he said, "We're going to take care of this at home, right?" I answered, "We already are." His breath is labored and shallow, and he is weak. Last night, before we even got comfortable in bed, his shirt and towel had to be changed three times because he was sweating buckets.

"Am I as sick as I look?" he asked last night. "Be honest," he said. And I was. I think he is starting to get how bad off he is. He's beginning to accept this. There isn't any drama or pain behind it, just a quiet internal energy, kind of solemn.

August 20

Since this last hospitalization, Stephan's strength has all but disappeared. Yesterday, he tried to get himself out of bed to take a shower and couldn't. I watched him trying and then quickly walked over and scooped him up, wrapping his arm around my shoulder, "How 'bout I help you today, hon?"

I walked him into the bathroom and sat him on the toilet while the water warmed up. I kept myself focused on what I had to do... check the water, grabbed a towel, and brought in Stephan's robe so that he wouldn't get cold.

I worked at not looking at him, or thinking about how defeated Stephan appeared. Then, as if I had done it a hundred times, I helped Stephan into the shower and told him to grab the little towel rack at the back of the shower. I soaped and rinsed him, had him lean his back onto my chest – head on my shoulder so I could wash his hair.

By the time I got Stephan out of the shower, his breath was heavy and he was looking weak. He sat on the toilet again as I dried him off and gave him a good shave (his skin is so loose now; I have to be extra careful not to cut him). The whole time, Stephan sat quietly, looking past me, his thoughts hidden behind a vacant stare. By the time I got him back into bed, I had a pounding headache.

I hate this fucking disease.

August 21

It's been a trying day to say the least. I decided to get up early, five A.M., to get some writing done. An experiment of sorts; nights haven't been too productive. I wrote for two hours straight, so I guess it worked pretty well, for today, anyway.

Meanwhile, Stephan has been feeling bad, and getting worse. It turns out he has been losing control of his bladder "just a little." He's not able to keep himself from pissing until he reaches the toilet. He said that last night that he ended up with a handful of piss before he made it to the bathroom. He feels completely humiliated. We both know it's only a matter of time before he needs to start wearing diapers. Just the thought of this is painful and horrifying.

In the middle of our conversation today, he began to feel nauseous. I helped him turn over and set up a trashcan, but the nausea passed. I held him and rocked him back and forth. Before I knew it, I was crying. I didn't want him to know, but I couldn't stop. I felt his hand on my head stroking my hair and that made me cry harder.

"This is really happening, isn't it?" I asked, sobbing as he patted my back and said we'd get through it. The fact that he was feeling bad and still comforting me only added to my tears.

Stephan turns 38 in a few days.

August 22

I'm trying this get up early routine again. I don't know who I'm kidding, thinking I can write. Especially in the middle of everything else happening around me. But I plod along at this idea of being a writer. If anything, at least it's a distraction.

Stephan wants nothing for his birthday. He has repeated this wish several times. I'm ignoring him. I don't know what to get him. What do you get for someone who is more than likely celebrating their last birthday? How do you make this day meaningful? Whatever it is I get will likely become my own. Do I get him something I really want? I'm going shopping this afternoon. I hope that I find something, somewhere that feels right.

After the bladder problem of the other day, Stephan did what he usually does. He became sullen and grouchy. "Everyone jokes about those old people diapers." I didn't know how to help him with this one. What do you say to someone who is losing the only thing he still had, his dignity? I just listened and tried to be as honest as I could. It was all I could offer.

But eventually, Stephan made some kind of peace with this whole thing because last night, he was much brighter. In fact, he talked about getting stronger and planning to be able to move around without any trouble.

Then it was my turn to be angry (although I didn't say anything to him). I didn't want to hear him talk like that. I didn't want to believe him; I didn't want him to believe his words either. Enough of this struggle! Enough of this valiant comeback shit!

I don't want to hope. I don't trust his words about his body. I want to get through the rest of this as quickly as possible. No more comebacks, no more talk about what's going to happen when he gets stronger. It doesn't last. It's not fair to talk like that – to me or to Stephan.

Still, I'll smile and listen to his words; I just can't believe them, anymore.

August 24

I gave Stephan his birthday present early. I figured it would be the only time we'd get together to celebrate it since his family would be over on his actual birthday. It wasn't much. I just bought a bottle of sparkling cider, flowers and an environmental tape of the ocean; hopefully it will help him relax.

When I gave it to him, I put it all together on his tray with some sandwiches. He looked sad, so helpless. There were tears in his eyes and his hand covered his mouth. He never got a complete sentence out, but I understood what he was trying to say.

We decided to save the cider until we could get time to be together (meaning that Stephan had more energy). The plan is to drink it and look through our photo album and relive the different things we've done over the past four years. Stephan said he has tried by himself several times but it is too hard. I don't know that it will be any easier for me.

Yesterday, Stephan's family showed up in full force to be with for his birthday. By the time I got home from work, they were all here, making an incredible amount of noise, and there was Stephan sitting at the table, looking somewhat sad and overwhelmed. He stayed up and talked with everyone for a long time, longer than he has in a while.

Eventually everyone left and I got him to bed, changed the dressing on his chest and turned off the light. As I did all of this, I was struck by how quiet the apartment was again. I thought to myself that no matter what people do, no matter how much they are "there" for me, the bottom line is… I'm in this alone.

It's just me who is turning out the light and making sure there are enough towels next to the bed for when Stephan sweats. I'm the one who gets him a fresh T-shirt or a glass of juice at three in the morning. I will be here, by myself tomorrow morning, wondering, making coffee, and getting ready for whatever happens next.

I'm not angry about this, just tired… tired, and scared.

August 25

Here we are now, two days after his birthday. Stephan is pretty exhausted from the long day yesterday. He's in bed resting (I hope). I've noticed him coughing again, that brief raspy cough from deep in the chest. He said it doesn't feel like pneumonia, but it doesn't sound too good, either.

There's nothing we can do about it; he's emphatic about not going back into the hospital, so we'll just go through our day, and I'll grit my teeth every time I hear that cough. Grit my teeth and hope, hope that the end is close.

MR. C

My first real taste of independence happened during the summer after I graduated high school. My family rented a house "down the shore," in Sea Isle City, New Jersey. I was working and planned to join everyone a day later, taking the bus from center city.

The first half of this trip involved a train ride into Reading Terminal, followed by a short walk from the train station to the bus terminal. As I walked through the city, I realized I was completely on my own. No one knew me; no one was expecting anything from me. In fact, I could do anything I wanted, and no one would know. I was a complete stranger and thrilled at the anonymity.

"No one would know," pulsed through my head as I walked down Thirteenth Street past a row of adult bookstores. "No one would know," my heart rate increasing, as I found myself looking at a blinking neon sign: A Bookstore with Class. I walked in, nerves on fire, half expecting an alarm to go off, or to be stopped and asked to identify myself.

Once inside I went into sensory overload. All of this blatant, raw, unapologetic sexuality – everywhere! I was frozen, in complete shock. Everywhere I looked, I saw penises. Well, there were also disgusting pictures of women with mouths opened wide enough to swallow a ham or palms under ridiculously large breasts, but my eyes kept focusing on the men these woman were pleasing. I was on the verge of orgasm from just standing in the middle of all that sex.

When I finally regained my composure, I followed my erection around the store, eventually finding the booths where, for the price of a quarter, you could catch two minutes of porn. Some of the booths offered gay porn, and I practically dove in headfirst. Those next two minutes felt like they went on forever. To see… to realize… that it was not only possible for two men to be together, but that they could enjoy it!

How could I not have known this was possible? I was looking at who I really was, and seeing HOW it looked, and there was no going back. I didn't want to go back.

Of course, I had no idea how to move forward. My mind played ping-pong the whole ride down the shore. My family... those men. My family... those men. As excited as I was, as clear as I was, I was terrified. I knew at some point I'd be leaving my family – I'd have to. There is no question in my mind about what my parents would say about a gay son.

I continued playing the game, and hid from my sexuality. I convinced myself all this gay stuff was experimental. After all, I still dated women. Every few months, though, I'd go to one of the adult bookstores outside my town and allow myself these guilt ridden 10-minute hand jobs in dark closets reeking of poppers and cum. It was all I could handle.

It was horrid, but it was a start. Every encounter was fired by this intense familiarity and such heavy, unnecessary guilt. I wanted so much to talk to these men, understand who they were, how they lived. I'd drive home from each encounter smoking a joint, or a cigarette – or both – and swear I'd never do it again, until the next time.

Then there was my straight "dating" I tried to do. At least I pretended to try. I'd hang out at parties, talk with my friends about the girls we knew, or the ones they wanted to meet. I flirted with girls in class, tell my friends I was building up the courage to ask them out, and then chicken out. One night, I called a girl from school for a date and sighed with relief when she said no.

Afterwards, I played the rejection card for a few months, pretending I was upset, and a little gun shy. And for a while, I could drop the game playing. But the, someone would start again with, "I have someone I want you to meet," or, "Why don't you ask out Caroline from Psych class?" I'd put on my game face – and act the part once again.

Like most of my siblings, I had to opt for the economical approach to my college education. Rather than live away from home, I took classes at one of Penn State's satellite campuses, Ogontz, about five miles away from where we lived. I always thought of it as an extension of high school; except there was more drinking and the classes were co-ed (my high school, Archbishop Wood, had separate boys and girls schools).

My parents were really good about not prying into our lives. They said that at 18 years of age, we were responsible for ourselves. Needless to say, I stopped going to church immediately. And while we certainly had more freedom, it was still my parents' house I was coming home to when the bars were closed and I was stumbling up the stairs in a drunken stupor.

I'd say it was a muffled freedom, with my sexuality bubbling constantly below the surface. Unfortunately, my first complete moment of undeniable independence would take another two years to arrive. It was the Holy Grail of my freedom: moving to State College.

Every August, I would watch my brothers and sister pack their things in the family car, getting ready to go away to school, and wondered at a world that took more than four hours to get to, a place where there were no parents watching, no siblings to hide from. I tried to picture myself walking around campus whenever I wanted, hanging in my dorm room – studying or not studying. I imagined the new friends I'd meet, the confidence I felt.

I was itching to know that kind of endless freedom. And I knew what I was going to do when the first night finally arrived: I was going to find a man and have sex. I didn't know how, I didn't know where, I just knew I would.

It was actually much easier than I expected.

I started the night at a party off campus with my sister and a bunch of people I knew from home. I figured I'd leave around midnight and cruise through town and hope for the best. There had to be at least one other gay man in this town. Somehow, when I announced that I was leaving, it was decided that several people would pile into a friend's car and bring me back into town. It was a drunken, noisy, five-minute trip that ended when I said, "Drop me off at the corner." I pushed myself numbly off someone's lap, and as I got out of the car, I grabbed for the nearest object to help steady myself. Hugging a parking meter, I laughed loudly as I watched them pull away.

It wasn't even one A.M., and the town was deserted since the semester wouldn't start for another few days (I was there, early for orientation). Like my solo trip into Philly a few years earlier, I felt like I could have been in the middle of anywhere. But this time, I wasn't going to find my parents waiting for me when I got home. I had my own dorm room and could stay out all night if I wanted. No one would know.

No one would know... that phrase whispered in my ear again. I was hundreds of miles away from anything familiar. The streets, the buildings, and the sounds – all of it seemed foreign, and I was very much alone. At 20 years of age, I had finally found a moment of complete isolation. I stood at the corner, holding onto the parking meter, swaying and listening to complete silence.

I finally made it.

When I started walking down College Ave, I wasn't sure where I was going. I just walked, watching myself walk. After a few blocks, I noticed a man turn a corner up ahead. He looked at me, and then started walking away. Several times, he turned back and looked directly at me. I lit a cigarette and followed him as he stepped behind a parking garage. There was a brief make-out session behind the building, and then we went to his home.

He was a music professor at Penn State. It was the first time I had sex with a man that wasn't hurried or hidden. It was the perfect ending to my first night of independence, and exactly what I had hoped it would be. I walked away from that experience more sure of who and what I was, yet I hid from it, hoping I'd eventually meet a woman who made me feel the same way.

For the next two years at State College, after partying with my friends, I'd cruise College Avenue on weekends hoping to meet other guys. It was probably the most painful, confusing time of my life. I couldn't see past the secrecy and the guilt. And I hadn't met one man who told me (or showed me) their life was good.

Once, I almost made it to a meeting of the gay student group, but the "what ifs" kept me from even walking in the building to see who made up

86

this group.

Then there was my education. While some of my classes were interesting, none felt especially challenging. I was getting honors but didn't feel especially inspired about what I was doing or learning. Still, I kept moving forward. Finish classes, get a job: That was the plan.

A job was the key to even more independence. It's what everyone else in my family was doing. I followed along, mostly because I didn't consider that there could be any other choices. I followed this logical progression because it was familiar and it was expected of me.

Truth be told, I was most happy when I worked at the restaurant during school breaks. I'd stay at either my sister's or a friend's apartment and work through to Christmas Eve, then take the bus home. The day after Christmas, I was back on the bus and headed to State College and a make believe life where I was on my own. Not that I did much more than work double shifts and watch MTV. But, I could smoke, walk around naked, and a few times, even have sex without any worry. Well, almost no worry. The sex part would be a source of worry for a long time – it just had a little more room to breathe.

Unfortunately, in spite of working weekends and over break – as well as two jobs over the summer months – I ran out of money. I'd spent it on an old VW Bug that required a ridiculous amount of money to get road worthy, and then, still had to be parked on a hill so that I could pop the clutch, since the battery was constantly dying. That car ruined me financially but achieved legendary status in my family.

It was towards the end of the fall semester, senior year, when I realized that I didn't have enough money to cover my tuition for spring term. I decided to take a year off and work at a restaurant near home, save money, and complete my student teaching the following spring at a school in the Philly area. My parents begged me to reconsider my plan. They could lend me the money, and I could finish on time. But my mind was made up and I had already made it clear – I wasn't going to borrow any money from them. I wasn't going to back out of that. I couldn't. I refused to graduate college and owe them money.

I moved home, bought a car, and got a job at a restaurant in the center of town. It was a tough adjustment being with my parents and after only a few months in my parents' house, I knew it was a mistake. I felt like I had taken a huge step back in my quest for independence.

When I heard that one of the cooks at the restaurant was looking for a roommate, I jumped at the chance. I remember Mom saying, "When we were your age, we lived with our parents until we were married. I don't understand why you feel you HAVE to move out." I kept my response simple, saying I just needed to prove something to myself. But in my mind, I was thinking, "I'd put off student teaching for TEN years if I had to. I would not stay in that house."

In spite of my parents' concern, everything moved ahead, as I had planned. The following spring, I started my student teaching assignment at school, down off Roosevelt Boulevard. My supervising teacher was very nice and supported me. But it was a tough class of kids with severe mental and emotional problems, and they were not having some wimpy wannabe teacher taking over. They challenged every limit I set, ran crying to the teacher when I didn't do things the way they liked, and generally ignored me when I tried to lead a lesson.

I was not having fun, and I questioned whether I really wanted to be a teacher. But it wasn't just the idea of being a teacher that was in question. I was confused about things much bigger than what my job was. I was finally connecting to that bigger notion; my sense of self. How could I make a decision about my career when there were more fundamental issues about who I was that needed a voice.

I will never forget it. I woke up one morning with about three weeks left in the semester and knew what I had to do. I made some coffee, packed a bag, and made the four hour drive to State College to meet with my advisor and drop out of the program. I still had enough credits to get my degree (I graduated – with honors even – with a B.S. in Education). But by dropping out of my student teaching, I wouldn't be certified, which meant that I would not be able to teach in the public school system – unless/until I finished my student teaching. I didn't care, as far as I was concerned, my teaching days were over.

I spent the next year and a half waiting tables. Well, waiting tables, and partying. What else does a twenty-something do with cash tips and a work schedule that doesn't start until four P.M.? No one in my family understood what I was doing. The questions circled around me for weeks: Why quit with three weeks only left? What's your plan? You're not going to wait tables for the rest of your life! What's going on?

What I knew but did not have the words for was that couldn't keep moving toward something I thought I was supposed to be. I didn't fit in the mold that my brothers, sisters and parents fit into. The college-marriage-family trifecta worked for them. For me, it always felt like I was wearing someone else's suit.

It was clear to me that I would have to sacrifice my relationship with my family in order to live the life I wanted, and that truth was paralyzing. I loved my family. I understood and accepted their faults, as they did mine. Any time we got together, we had fun. I know how much they all loved me. But there was only one way this would go; my challenge was to figure out how to get there.

How lucky we are that the universe has a great sense of humor and listens to the prayers you keep secret – even from yourself.

Two years after I walked away from the world of education, I got a call from Anita, a former classmate from Penn State who was teaching in Philly. We had quite a history during our college days, finding ourselves at more than one party fucked up and jamming to Bruce or the Stones. I remember on party in particular at her apartment, where I said I was too stoned to walk to the bathroom, and decided to crawl down the hall as Anita threw rose petals on the floor in front of me. She was one of the few people who made life at State College bearable. I lost touch with her when I quit student teaching.

When I answered the phone, Anita, in that typical Philadelphian way of hers, said, "Hey Ter, it's Aneeeda." A long breath, and then, "Listen, here's the deal. I'm teaching at this school in West Oak Lane, St. Ignatius Elementary School. Ever hear of it?" Before I opened my mouth to answer, she continued, "Doesn't matter. Let me tell ya what's going on. One of the Seventh grade teachers quit today. Out o' th' blue. She was this little woman, kind of tense, ya know, with thin lips and bad shoes. Anyways… she stood up in front of class today after morning prayers and shouted, 'You kids are IMPOSSIBLE… I QUIT!' Someone told me during faculty lunch that Anthony Brown farted. She quit cuz one o' her kids passes gas. Whatever. Next thing we know, Sister Ann Marie, she's the principal, (whispers) the staff all calls her SAM... holds this emergency staff meeting at lunch and asks us if we know someone who would be able to step into the Seventh grade position, pronto. And I thought of you. You interested?"

As I moved my lips to form an answer, she continued, "I'll tell you the truth. This class DOES have a bad reputation – since day one, apparently. They need someone who can give them a little structure and listen. It's a great school. Did I tell you it's an all-Black school? Most of the staff? We're white. And the kids – they are so sweet! The rest of the staff is great. This is my second year here, and I love it. You will, too. What do you think? Still want to be a teacher?"

All I could say was, "Anita. Me? A Catholic school? Religion classes?" But she wouldn't take no for an answer. Two minutes later, I was scheduling a meeting with the principal, Sister Ann Marie, (a.k.a. SAM), for the next morning at 10:00 A.M., "right after morning mass."

I wasn't so sure I was really up for this, but I figured I had nothing to lose. I had to close the restaurant that night, which meant not getting home until about 2:30 A.M. I figured I could still get five hours sleep, wake up, make some strong coffee in the morning, and I'd be good to go.

When I got home from work that night, I had a beer, smoked a bowl, and wandered to my bedroom around 3:00 A.M. I lay in bed, in that soft, sweet space right before sleep claims you, when I thought I felt something on my leg. I couldn't decide if it was real or not. I shifted a little and let go a little more, only now realize that the little thing on my leg was definitely real. Before I could figure out exactly what it was, I felt an electric shock pierce my calf. STING!

"What the FUCK!" I screamed as I lunged for the light switch. Once my eyes adjusted, I saw this twitching bee crawling around in my sheets. I grabbed a tissue and squeezed it tightly around that little sucker until I felt the pleasant squish of revenge, and flushed it down the toilet.

When I climbed back into bed, it was 3:45 A.M. With luck, I could still manage four hours of sleep. Then I just had to hold it together for a little while, act nice for the sister, and I could come home for a nap before I had to go and close the restaurant again. It took a while, but eventually, my heart rate slowed down, and I could feel myself slipping away, when suddenly, STING! STING! STING!

"Fucking FUCK!" I screamed as I jumped out of bed. This time, when I snapped on the light, I found three bees moving across my sheets. It was like something out of the Twilight Zone.

Still stoned and now, totally wired, the best I could do was grab my alarm clock and head to the couch. At that point, if I could catch even an hour of sleep, it would have been a miracle. I lay there wondering what SAM was like, and fell into a restless sleep during which I dreamed that SAM was a bee. She was sitting at her desk interviewing me, but her stinger kept sliding towards me from under the desk, scratching my leg. When the alarm went off at 8:00 A.M., I was already awake. There were three huge welts on my left leg; my eyes felt like they'd been rolled in sandpaper; and my neck, which had been pressed sideways into the couch's wooden armrest, wasn't too happy when I pulled myself vertical.

There was no way I could reschedule this interview – it just was not an option. Besides, I was pretty sure that I was going to get the job. How could I not? It was the end of September. Where else was SAM going to find someone? Desperation was on my side. I just had to get there and be somewhat human.

I showered, shaved, iron my shirt, threw back some eye drops, and chugged a few cups of strong coffee. I was driving to the interview when I began to think about actually being a teacher and what it would look like. I suddenly felt as if I had something to prove, at least to myself. I stubbed out my cigarette and reached into my glove compartment for my mouthwash. At the next traffic light, I took a big swig and swished it around, spitting it out window when I got the green.

When I pull into the parking lot of St. Ignatius Elementary School, I saw who I could only assume was SAM, standing at the door. She had a slightly mannish look about her, with short-cropped salt and pepper hair and posture as rigid as a flagpole. Her white habit was pulled so tightly around her waist I wondered if she could breathe. But it was her face that made me almost continue driving right out the exit.

There was no light behind her eyes, just a black fire filled with impatience. I felt like I was in trouble already, and I didn't even know what I had done wrong. In spite of myself, or perhaps a delayed reaction to the bee stings, my heart was pounding in my chest. I was afraid she would make me call my parents to tell them about the half-smoked joint hidden in the ashtray.

My "interview" was really an orientation. SAM's movements were crisp and military. She made it clear that discipline would be my best tool in dealing with this class. As we walked quickly down the hallway, I was hit with that familiar smell of crayons, floor wax and dusty sunshine only found in school. She handed me stacks of lesson plans and led me to my new classroom, where a pile of un-graded tests was added to the pile. I had a two-second review of the subjects I would teach, told where I could find chalk, and reminded what time I was expected in the schoolyard Monday morning.

Then she looked squarely at me and said, "This class is a wild bunch, Terry. They need firm LIMITS. They don't need a friend. Am I understood?"

"Absolutely, Sister" I responded, "I will do my best." And hoped against hope it would be good enough.

It was the news my parents had been waiting for. I was finally settling down, growing up. The fact that I would be teaching in a Catholic grade school only made the news even better for them. I quickly squelched any hopes they had at my complete redemption by saying, "And get this...I have to teach religion! How's that for ironic?"

I knew they were worried about me, though they kept any concerns to themselves. I could feel them watching nervously whenever I visited. In their minds, I was still not living up to my potential. In my mind, I was still trying to understand my potential. But this teaching job... it gave them (and me) hope.

I loved everything about that year, even SAM and her domineering, severe approach to running the school. She was a throwback to the nuns of my youth, literally pulling children out of their seats, the dramatic screaming tirades, red-faced and out of control. She was cold and bitter, and when I wasn't afraid of her, I felt sad for her.

I decided it was my job to lighten things up in my classroom and with my fellow teachers. And believe me, as my mother would say, "I gave her a run for her money."

SAM was all about control; I was more about expression. She scolded me in front of the class in the middle of my first supervision because I allowed my students to answer questions without raising their hands. "You can't let these kids walk all over you," she said, throwing the same look of impatience at me that she levied on the kids.

I didn't think I was letting the kids walk all over me. I believed that I was giving them a space where they could relax. SAM saw that as weakness, surrender. We eventually had a truce built around the unspoken assumption that this was a one-year commitment. We both knew I wouldn't be returning the next year.

I tried to keep a slightly tighter rein on the class, and she appeared a little less judgmental. One time at the end of recess, after SAM sharply reminded me to keep my class in control as they lined up to go inside, one of the kids said, "Don't worry Mr. C., she just up tight. It ain't yo fault. My momma say, 'For a woman of God, she be awful angry.'"

My seventh grade partner and I split teaching responsibilities. She covered history and geography; I got the math and science. I'm not sure how it happened, but I was also the lucky one responsible for teaching the section on sex education.

SAM quite often used the school intercom system to listen in on different classes, sometimes interrupting in the middle of a lesson like some omniscient being, "Mr. Connell," her voice booming out of the intercom and startling everyone into attention, "Mr. Connell, could you have someone in the class summarize what you just said about mitosis? Given the voices I hear in the background, I'm not convinced everyone was paying attention!"

As I set up the filmstrip to begin the sex education class, I wondered if SAM would listen in and decided not to think too much about it. If SAM wanted to listen in as I rolled through the filmstrip while reading accompanying text and doing my best to show some level of ease around words like vagina and testicles, I was not going to stop her.

It was a strange, incredible convergence of events: me, a closeted, sexually repressed gay man, teaching sex education in a Catholic elementary school to a group of inner city kids. What are the chances? As a teacher, my intention was to treat my students with respect and to give them freedom to express themselves. So it should have been no surprise when one of the boys raised his hand and asked quite sincerely, "Why do girls be smellin' like fish like they do?"

Fortunately, one of the girls was already taking care of the question before I could even blink, "That's cuz they don't clean themselves. That's nasty!" In a million years, I wouldn't have come up with a better answer.

When the anatomical cartoon of intercourse flashed on the screen, I heard one of the nerdy kids squeak from behind me, "You mean that's it? You just stick it in there?" Again, I was saved by the quick wit and intelligence of my students. From somewhere further back one of the boys shouted, "No man. You wanna move it around cuz it feel GOOD!"

Since my salary teaching at a Catholic school was less than half of what I was making as a waiter and bartender, I decided to keep two shifts a week at the restaurant – Tuesday and Saturday nights. It was exhausting, but I really didn't have a choice. My tips from those two nights doubled my income. It also kept me in touch with my friends who were still working at the restaurant. Saturday nights, if we all finished early enough, I'd invite a few people back to my apartment where we'd drink beer, smoke a joint or two and they'd help me grade papers. They got a kick out of my "real" job and loved to see what lessons I was working on, or how SAM was tormenting me.

By the end of the year, I came to realize that I was a good listener and my strengths were better suited to one-on-one and small group settings than teaching math and coordinating lesson plans. I was right to stop my student teaching. I didn't like teaching. I was, at best, an adequate teacher. But, I finished the year with a new plan and a new sense of optimism. I would go back to school and study to be a therapist.

AIDS Timeline #6

April 8, 1990: Ryan White dies of AIDS-related complications.

October, 1990: A national Speak-Out by women with AIDS is held in Washington, D.C. to protest Social Security definitions of disability, which discriminate against women and people of color. A few months later, ACT Up Women's Caucus protests and testifies at the CDC, calling for an expansion of the AIDS definition.

By the **end of 1990**: 198,466 people in the U.S. are diagnosed with AIDS. 121,255 are dead from the disease.

November 4, 1991: Lead singer of Queen, Freddie Mercury, joins a growing list of celebrities to die from AIDS. Others celebrities include: Alvin Ailey, Rock Hudson, Rudolf Nureyev, and Liberace.

At the **1991 Tony Awards**, the red ribbon is introduced as the international symbol of AIDS awareness by Broadway Cares/Equity Fights AIDS and Visual AIDS.

August 26

I don't understand how days fold into each other so quickly, and so little seems to change, except that it's another day, and we've survived. Stephan's stomach is bothering him more. He's made an appointment with the "AIDS specialist" at Graduate Hospital for tomorrow. I don't know why, really. Whatever they find, Stephan says he's not going into the hospital, and he's not doing any kind of radiation or chemotherapy.

"What's the point?" I asked, Stephan but he really didn't have an answer. This morning he still felt pretty bad. I tried getting someone to cover my shift but couldn't. Luckily, a friend called and said she could stay with Stephan, so I got ready for work. Stephan and I shower together regularly now. Sometimes he feels like a rag doll when I'm holding him up. He just lets his head flop against my shoulder as I rinse the shampoo out of his hair.

He's always so grateful after I've dried him and gotten him back to bed. I never knew that one's heart could be torn open with sadness and beauty, all at once. Again, and again. Over, and over.

I dried his hair and brushed his teeth, and there on the bed we made love in a way I had never thought possible. Every movement was giving, so honest. It was about being with each other, remembering how we could be together.

August 29

Stephan's appointment with the specialist seemed to be a good one. The pain Stephan's been feeling in his stomach is most likely related to constipation. He's full of shit! Go figure. Now he's got to take five days of a serious laxative that will, I hope relieve the pain.

There is a possibility that it is related to the lymph nodes (cancer), but since Stephan refuses any kind of surgery or treatment, that's a question that will go unanswered.

We also learned that Stephan has lost ten pounds. It doesn't sound like much when you talk about it, but it is obvious. He looks like one of those AIDS patients I've seen in magazines or on TV. We're going to try to fatten him up a little bit – should be an interesting little trick in the middle of this laxative treatment.

We had the nicest night last night. It was just Stephan and me. No one came over, no one called. It was quiet, relaxing, wonderful. For a while, it felt almost "normal." We didn't talk about AIDS, didn't worry about what might happen. Instead, we pretended that all was right in our world. It felt great!

Stephan and I took a walk today. The sun was warm and a breeze blew just strong enough to keep us from being hot as we walked. This was the first time Stephan went out in public using a cane. He asked if I was embarrassed to be with him. I found the question amusing; he was completely serious. "Of course not," I said. "Are you?" "I don't know what I am," he said as we continued our walk.

September 1

Every night as we are getting ready for bed, there is a moment when the lights are turned off that I feel completely at peace. I take Stephan's hand in mine and remind myself how important love is, and how lucky I am, and for a second or two, everything moves away, and we are suspended above it all.

Then, I start to think.

I can't help myself. My mind grabs at a passing thought, spins it around, tosses it away and immediately, another holds my attention, refusing to let go. Everything from the electric bill, to my smoking, to the laundry in the dryer, to whatever I imagine will happen next week.

Breath in. Breath out. I try to get myself to let go of everything and relax. Breath in. Breath out. Don't think about money; everything will work out. Breath in. What about when things get worse here and Stephan's needing more and more care? Breath out. Breath in. Breath out. Breath in. I need to find a better job. Breath out.

Eventually, I'm able to put this angst away and fall asleep. Some nights are easier than others. Last night took a little more effort than usual. I'm worried about our money situation and Stephan seems to have hit a plateau. His health hasn't gotten any worse, and it certainly hasn't gotten any better either.

Right now, the biggest problem continues to be his stomach. He has pain and feels nauseous and his stomach gets really distended.

My theory is that he has become reliant on the Percocet and the pains are his body needing more. He's been taking them daily for two months now. It's hard to imagine that he hasn't become dependent on them. I suggested that he talk to his doctor about this, but he hasn't yet.

He asked me not to leave him alone last night. For three hours, I held him, wiped the sweat off him, and listened to him talk about almost anything that came to his mind. I heard about dreams he's been having (mostly about putting his life in order), his feelings about his nephew, the TV show we watched last night, the importance of being complete with people, money. I hardly said a word, until the money subject came up, of course.

Later, as I was getting ready for bed, I found myself suddenly feeling angry. No apparent reason, just angry: angry at Stephan for being sick; angry that I did a better job brushing his teeth than he could; angry that we were having money problems, angry that he was still here making life difficult, and suddenly, really angry that my family was ignorant to all of it. It came over me so quickly that it startled me. I poured some whiskey, grabbed the rest of the joint from the ashtray, and took a seat on the windowsill.

September 8

I don't know what happened, but Stephan has been acting strange lately. He was up and out of the house two days in a row. And, he usually needs a few days to recoup after exerting himself, but that hasn't happened either. Who knows? Maybe it won't. Is it possible that he is regaining strength? Again, I find myself selfishly hoping not.

I feel myself getting resentful and losing my patience. More and more, I have to talk myself into this mindset of acceptance, of letting go. The thought of our lives playing out like this for another year is paralyzing. I hate not being able to do what I want. I've been preparing myself for something that may actually be much farther off than I had anticipated, and this scares the shit out of me. How do I live the life I want when I am with someone who won't let go?

If Stephan were to read these words, he'd tell me to get over it and do what I want. It only it was that easy.

September 9

Whatever was going on as I was writing last night stayed with me this morning. I was in a horrible mood. I kept playing the same tape over and over in my head. I got more and more angry and realized that I felt betrayed by Stephan. He was looking better, had energy and was talking about different treatments his doctor suggested. This is the man who told me he didn't want any more medicine and was ready to deal with everything on his own.

I came home tonight and tried to allow myself to be with Stephan, to enjoy his company, his grace. When I can keep it in that moment, everything is fine, at least for the moment; even the prospect of his death. I asked what he thinks about his life three, maybe five months from now. He didn't know how to respond.

He asked me the same question and I told him I was expecting his death. I said I didn't trust what was happening now that was giving him this "energy." I was glad to see him feeling better, but I didn't trust it.

"You're just waiting for me to die, aren't you?" he asked me. I hesitated for a moment and shrugged. "Sometimes," I said.

How could I not? Here's what's going on, in addition to AIDS and anemia and the repeated bouts of pneumonia and ongoing stomach issues: Stephan has been diagnosed with a type of tuberculosis common among AIDS patients - he'll be taking two medications to treat this. Syphilis has also shown up in his blood tests. He had it years ago, and the doctor thinks it reappeared because of the HIV. Stephan is not symptomatic (it's kind of like Herpes). To treat the syphilis, he will get a series of six shots over the next few weeks. His doctors are also going to discuss the option of inserting a permanent port for his IV treatments.

September 10

There is this guilt following me since I wrote the last two entries. It's hard not to fall into it. I guess that's part of this whole fucked up experience. I'm assuming I'm not unique in wanting death to come sooner than later (I hope I'm not). This guilt is also amplified by the fact that Stephan is not feeling well this morning.

His stomach is giving him trouble, and he didn't sleep well last night. Now he is resting, I hope.

I can't describe what it feels like is to see him like this. It never stays the same. I know it's wrong, but I was relieved, relieved because maybe he really is sicker than he appeared just a few days ago. Then, I got worried. What if Stephan IS getting worse? How will we get through?

I feel like I am a ping-pong ball going back and forth from one set of thoughts and emotions to another. Everything is out of control. And somehow, in the middle of it, I keep going through my day... laundry, shower, work, look in on Stephan, have a cigarette. Repeat.

I found refuge the past couple of days in a new story I'm working on. It's a difficult story to write. Everything sounds much better in my head. I keep plugging along, and sometimes I feel myself relax and find a groove. Stephan likes it so far.

September 15

Mom called today. She wanted to know how things were going, and to let me know she and Dad were thinking about me. I didn't have much to say. It's always a struggle, wondering how much to share – how honest to be. It always seems easier to keep our conversation safe, to aim for the middle. I didn't talk about how worried I am about our money situation. I decided not to mention how frustrating life is for me. It's hard to talk about my life with a man they won't recognize, a life they don't see.

I walked around town yesterday and watched people on their way to wherever... faces relaxed, happily moving through life, expecting more of the same tomorrow. I watched this couple walk to their car and I became acutely aware of how unhappy I am. How hollow and lost.

It feels like this hell has been going on forever. It's a nail-biting, worried existence. I can't remember the last time I've been totally comfortable, relaxed. I miss it, and I know it isn't coming my way any time soon. I keep walking and try to stay present to each moment. Still, even in those moments when I can let go, I always feel this undertow that stays near and pulls at my heart and reminds me not to enjoy myself too much.

Lately, I feel obligated more than I feel inspired by love. This is not a good feeling, and I end up resentful and fantasizing about a future of freedom and fun. Over the past week I had at least three different dreams involving sex. In each one, a man tries to seduce me. I allow him to go only so far and then I stop because I think of Stephan. But those few moments are wild, sexy, uninhibited. It's nice to feel alive in that way again – even if it is in my head.

Stephan sees the doctor tomorrow. He's afraid he's addicted to Percocet. I think he probably is and wonder what difference does it makes. The pain in his abdomen is more acute and is restricted to one place, by his left rib. Then there's the usual stuff he's got going on. I don't expect anything too revealing from this appointment, though it's hard to predict anything anymore.

September 18

I have the evening off and the perfect opportunity to concentrate on my writing, but I feel restless. It's even a struggle to sit here and write this. Not that there is anything new: It's just another day in the life of uncertainty. In my last three shifts, I have made less than $150. Rent is due in ten days, and I don't have enough to cover it. I don't know if I will.

The results of the doctor appointment: the port will be put in Monday; Stephan will be receiving regular Pentam treatments as a protective measure against pneumonia. His hemoglobin is low, and they want to give him three pints of blood. Stephan is refusing. He said the last time he got a transfusion he was sick for days and didn't feel any better.

He's also taking new antibiotics for this Tuberculosis-like thing he's got, and Penicillin once a week for the next three weeks to fight any Syphilis that may still be in his system.

Life is getting increasingly hard, and there is no sign of it getting any easier. I try to trust that things are moving in the right direction, and in some strange way, I'm sure they are.

MENTAL HEALTH TECHNICIAN

I was always a big believer in the idea that change brings about change, so I wasn't all that surprised to see how my year as a teacher sent ripples of change through my life. Since I had to be at school and on my game before eight each morning, I stopped partying during the week. Not too long after I started teaching, I quit smoking cigarettes, and, for the first time in my life, started paying attention to my health.

I began running around a track at the end of my block. First it was a lot of walking with short bursts of light jogging in between, but gradually I increased my mileage, and after a few months I was doing three, sometimes five miles, a couple of times a week. On my runs, I would pass a Tae Kown Do school not too far from my apartment. One day at the end of my run, I stopped in and asked about classes. I decided it was time I learned how to defend myself and maybe throw a punch without looking like my little sister.

I showed up for my first beginner's class only to discover that my other classmates included seven kids around the age of ten and an older woman (maybe 35) who was going through a divorce. I stood there towering above everyone, feeling a bit like Jerry Lewis as I went through my first set of punching drills, trying to sound as aggressive and confident as I could while flinging my right fist forward, "Haah!" Left fist, "Haah!" Right, "Haah!"

Our instructor was a tall, powerful looking man from Trinidad with dark skin and a loud, commanding voice. I winced a little as he came over to me, expecting laughter and the usual "lady/boy" insults I'd heard a thousand times before. Instead, he adjusted my hand and forearm, emphasizing the forward motion of the first two knuckles. We continued, "Haah!" and he made the same adjustment on the other side.

Then, again, "Haah!" With a clinical eye, he kept pulling and pushing my bones into place. Then he stopped the class and asked, "Do you see what's happening? You can't let your wrist collapse. There's more efficiency in the action when the bones of your wrist line up with your arm. You have more power, because now your whole upper body is involved. Try again."

And just like that, I got it. He didn't want to ridicule me. He wasn't interested in how embarrassed I was. He didn't care that these were the first real aggressive movements I'd ever allowed myself. He was interested in my form, and he was interested in my effort. That was it. It didn't matter what they called me on the baseball field when I was nine years old. He was there to teach. He wanted to know if I could listen to the instructions, make an effort to improve?

I said goodbye to my history as a failed jock, and for the next year and half, showed up twice a week with my whites on, belt tied perfectly, and worked as hard as I could. It was exhausting, and thrilling. I progressed steadily, amazing myself over and over at how much I liked it, and how good I was getting. I finally understood what it felt like to be an athlete.

There was a time in my early twenties when I was able to split a board in half, doing a reverse jump-kick. Crazy, I know. But, it was a huge breakthrough in my training, and to this day, when I stop to think about it, I can remember everything about the first time I landed that kick.

I had my blue belt and was taking the test for my red stripe. I had already missed my first two attempts at this kick and was feeling a bit defeated. I was tired from a difficult sparring match not five minutes earlier and trying to ignore the roomful of people watching me. As I got ready for my last attempt, I was already assuming I'd miss, consoling myself for trying hard, when my teacher, shouted from across the room, "C'mon Terry, focus."

And like that, I looked at the board, took a quick breath, and jumped. As I was jumping, I knew this one would land correctly. Like a slow motion sequence from a martial arts movie, I watched myself pull my right knee up, turn mid-air, extend my heel, and slam it through the board with a loud, "Heyaahhh!" When I landed, I heard my teacher say, "Thank you," matter-of-factly, and call the next student.

A few weeks later, while sparring with one of the black belts during class, I decided it was time to end my Tae Kwon Do training. He was fast, and very aggressive. The best I could do was continually back away and block whatever was coming at me. Mr. Cyrus was shouting cues, "Footwork... watch your breathing, Terry... follow through on your punches..." I was literally getting my ass kicked and I wasn't having fun. When my opponent landed a kick in my side ribs that sent me flying across the room, all I could think was, "I'm done." I moved around, for the rest of the match, faking a few kicks, just trying to ride out the clock. I didn't want to retaliate.

I didn't care who won. I wasn't interested in defeating anyone. I had learned more than I had expected, and it was time to stop. I finished that class and never went back.

With SAM and St. Ignatius behind me, it was time to start plotting my way towards grad school. I returned to waiting tables but also began looking for a job that would help me get experience on my path to becoming a therapist. I didn't realize how hard it would be. There was little to choose from – mostly residential positions in halfway houses with rough kids falling through the system until they were finally old enough to go to jail. I may have felt more like an athlete, but I wasn't interested in testing my fighting skills at work.

Most of the other counseling positions required experience or were Master's level. When I saw "Mental Health Technician" across the top of an ad for The Horsham Clinic, I couldn't imagine what that job title meant. I imagined people in navy blue overalls giving advice as they changed the oil and checked the wheel alignment. Mental Health Technician – at a psychiatric hospital – it sounded cold and regimented, like something you'd find at the Sears Psychiatry Center.

In the 1980s, in-patient psychiatric treatment was a common way to treat children who were out of control. Managed care hadn't found its way into the field of mental health yet, and insurance companies were paying for three, four, even six months of in-patient treatment. The Horsham Clinic was one of the better facilities in the area, and a Mental Health Technician only needed a bachelor's degree to apply, experience was "preferred." When I spoke with Human Resources and learned they offered tuition reimbursement, I was convinced this was the right job for me.

The job description was something like this: A Mental Health Technician's responsibilities include: supervising fifteen to thirty adolescent, psychiatric patients during a variety of different scheduled activities, recording attendance every 15 minutes (patients have been known to "elope" from different activities, some actually escaping off grounds, while most are caught and brought back), assisting allied staff (teachers, recreation therapists, art therapists) during unit activities, establishing limits and enforcing rules of the unit, and during free time, provide one-on-one counseling focused on issues and goals identified when the patient was admitted.

I was sold. I wanted this job and spent a lot of time preparing for the interview. Somehow, I had to explain a resume that featured only nine months of professional teaching experience. But how do I account for the two years I had spent before teaching smoking copious amounts of pot, drinking until all hours, and indulging an anxious, homophobic sense of self?

I sat in the lobby waiting for my interview feeling the way I used to feel before I went to Confession: like I was going to get caught. When the Margaret Flannery, a middle-aged, heavy-set woman came out to introduce herself as Adolescent Unit Nursing Coordinator, I knew I had nothing to worry about. Irish Catholic mothers are easy to read. Margaret gave me a familiar smile as we sat down to talk. We talked about the job description, the schedule, and my plans for grad school. Then Margaret, looking up from my application, said, "You went to Archbishop Wood? Do you have a brother who graduated from Wood in 1977?" It turned out that one of Margaret's sons had graduated with one of my brothers. In fact, Margaret knew my parents and had spent more than one high school football or basketball game in the bleachers talking with them. Who would have thought that I'd be thankful for my Irish Catholic background?

In reality, though, just being a man would probably have gotten me the job. Some of the boys on the adolescent unit were over six feet tall, easily weighing fifty or sixty pounds more than most of the nurses. Margaret was always on the lookout for male applicants. Some, she said, didn't work out "for all kinds of reasons..." then she patted my hand, as we left our meeting with Dr. Small, the clinical director of the unit. "But you... you're going to be just fine."

In the orientation for my new job as Mental Health Technician, I learned about the patients on the Adolescent Unit. Most signed in voluntarily, presenting with all kinds of problems, suicide attempts, eating disorders, drug use, sexual acting out, violent behavior, and more than a few kids with psychotic and schizophrenic diagnoses. It wasn't uncommon for kids to lose control and have to be wrestled to the ground, sometimes put in four-point-restraints in the "Seclusion Room." So a large portion of my orientation was spent in role-play situations, practicing over and over the right dialogue to use when a patient starts to escalate; when and how to signal coworkers for assistance; and how to physically restrain a patient and get them into four-point restraints.

Consistency and teamwork were the two words emphasized over and over during orientation. Coming from a family of eleven, they were two words I was familiar with. "Consistency and teamwork," I chanted to myself as I drove in on my first day. When Margaret introduced me to the unit during Morning Meeting, I smiled weakly at 24 teens and for a brief moment, I felt as naked as when I played Jesus on the cross years ago.

Consistency and teamwork, I thought as I watched these kids look through me in my chinos and blue Oxford. I suddenly felt like I was swimming with sharks, and I wondered if maybe I had jumped in the deep end a little too quickly.

But that's what makes teamwork so important to this job. I had to remember that I wasn't dealing with any of this alone. I had twelve people around me, all working toward the same goal, using the same approach. I looked around the room at the men and women on my team, and hoped I could rise to whatever challenges I was thrown. I was warned more than once in orientation that I'd be tested. The patients were manipulative and were constantly trying to play one staff member against another. "Don't forget, it's a psych hospital. These patients are here for a reason. Don't take anything they say at face value. And they will try all kinds of tricks to rope you in and get their way."

This is where consistency came in to play. The rules were in place for a reason. They are enforced regardless of the story a patient told. Most of these kids on the Adolescent Unit were experts at getting what they wanted.

For them, rules had no meaning, let alone consequences. One of the most important concepts a patient learned on the adolescent unit was to be held accountable for his behavior. And one of the most important aspects of a Mental Health Technician's job was to be sure the kids were following the rules and to be consistent in handing out consequences when rules were broken.

Cursing, lateness, and disobeying staff were all minor infractions that resulted in "room time," which meant an hour in their rooms without music and, worst of all for them. More extreme behaviors resulted in more extreme consequences. This system didn't just focus on negative behaviors. Patients earned privileges (free time in the Rec Room, weekend passes, later bed time) when they followed rules and showed progress in their treatment.

There was structure to the schedule: These kids were on some kind of therapeutic activity from eight in the morning until seven each night. I thought it was a well-designed program, and as nervous as I was, I was curious to see how it all worked. Twenty minutes into my first day on the job, I got my answer.

I was making rounds, moving from one bedroom to another, checking to make sure beds were made, rooms in order, and everyone was ready for breakfast. When I walked into Ron's room, he was staring out the window, clothes and towels in a pile around him. I said, "Ron, you've got less than five minutes to get your stuff together, or you know you get an hour of room time and have to stay on the unit for breakfast."

He looked up at me and laughed. "Fuck you!"

And just like that, I was calling the rest of the staff over and asking Ron to walk with us to the Seclusion Room. "I didn't DO nothin'!" he shouted, punching a wall, which got him five hours of room time and loss of off unit activities until he met with his psychiatrist. I was working to control my shaking voice. "Last chance, Ron," I said. "You can walk with us to…" and in a rush, he tried to run past me, and my coworkers.

We had him pinned to the floor in no time, his shouts echoing down the unit hall. Ron squirmed and cursed the whole time we carried him back to the Seclusion Room, where the charge nurse was already waiting, medication in one hand, clipboard and pen in the other. We carried Ron over to the bed, and she took over. "Ron, if you can't gain some control, we're going to put you in four points. I've got your meds here, if you think it will help. What's it going to be?" There were a few more seconds of resistance before he stopped bucking, and slowly, two of us let go. A few more seconds, his back muscles softened, and the other staff let go. Ron then collapsed on the bed and covered his face, crying uncontrollably.

Later, during the rehash, Margaret again patted my hand and asked if I was okay. We talked about how much of this was a result of the family therapy session Ron had later, and how much was a test. "Either way, you handled it just right," Margaret clucked, a bit like a proud mother. The charge nurse agreed. "It was actually a good introduction to the unit. You KNOW everyone was wondering what you're made of. Now, they know." I think my old boss, SAM, would have been very impressed.

That first day set the tone for the rest of my time on the Adolescent Unit. I became known as a bit of a hard ass – who would have guessed? The kids respected me for it. It was a turning point for me. At 25 years of age, I had finally learned to access the "masculine" part of who I was, my power. For the longest time, I had denied that I had any. My fear of my sexuality had completely negated any sense of my masculinity. But with a few years of martial arts training, and not living with my parents I was slowly shedding those layers of insecurity and self-doubt that I had used to shield the most genuine parts of myself from the strict, narrow world-view of my parents.

To have a team of professionals welcome me, and respect me as an equal was the confirmation I didn't know I was looking for.

I became a sponge, sitting in on art therapy and psychodrama sessions as often as I could, amazed at how the therapists could create an activity and generate the most insightful conversations following it. I watched in complete awe one afternoon as the art therapist was able to help a hardened, drug-abusing sixteen-year-old to drop his defenses and talk about how his parents' divorce affected him. It was so profound, so powerful, and so delicate.

After recreation therapy, I would talk with the therapists about what they saw during the session – connecting a patient's reckless behavior during a team activity with the way he treated his family. I couldn't get enough. Group dynamics, body language, the flow of energy during an activity were all effective ways of helping patients understand themselves and whatever had brought them to the psych unit. When a depressed patient hears from his peers how his behavior affects the group, it's more effective than any conversation a parent might have with him. When a group can work together and provide a space where breakthroughs are reached, it heals in the most amazing ripples and layers.

During my time on the Adolescent Unit, I sat with patients placed on 24-hour suicide watch more than once. It was a great way to make time-and-a-half, and when the right night nurse was on, I could take two-hour naps in one of the social worker's offices between two-hour shifts of just sitting and watching someone sleep in four point restraints.

I saw more than one kid go through psychotic breaks, and I watched as one obsessive-compulsive girl worked through a complicated tapping routine every time she left her room – three times on the door, twice on her arm, three traced circles around the handle topped off with a quick tap of her right elbow when the door was finally closed. Sometimes, patients would try to run away, which was always an adventure, since the hospital sat on an old farm and was surrounded by acres of fields flanked by thick groves of trees.

There were kids who scrubbed their genitals raw, and hid drugs up their asses or inside toothpaste containers. I sat with girls who had eating disorders as they struggled to eat the whites of an egg for breakfast, and watched in shock as varsity athletes consumed by rage at their demanding fathers collapsed on the floor in tears after a difficult family therapy session.

Being a Mental Health Technician was five years of non-stop, on the job training. These were exactly the kind of kids I wanted to work with: Depressed, misunderstood, angry, and ignored. I believed I could help them, felt sure I was moving into a career where I could succeed.

When the psychiatrists on the unit started commenting on my notes, or requested that I sit in on the next session, I felt pride, a knowing satisfaction. There really was a future for me in this field. I had instinct and a good way of communicating to this population. That I was looking *at myself in these displaced, wounded faces wouldn't be clear to me for a long while.*

I was accepted into Temple University's Master's Program in Counseling Psychology and began taking classes. I decided to focus on family and group therapy as specialties and arranged my classes and practicum placements in that direction.

School had a very different feel to it this time around. I wasn't choosing a career to "fall back on," I wasn't following someone else's plan of what my life should look like. I had found a focus and a passion. I knew I was on the right path, because it was a path I had chosen.

And finally, I found a therapist and began to actually talk with someone else about the worries I felt around my sexuality and my relationship with my family. It was time for me to stop hiding from them. Coming out was the last step, my final hurdle. It paralyzed me to look at my future and not see my family in it. But I knew where the gay thing landed in the Faith Trumps Family scale.

It would take another two years, and meeting Stephan, before I finally decided to tell the truth. So much worry, so much anger... it was immobilizing. And, from my point of view, it was inevitable: A faith that trumps family, divides it.

AIDS Timeline #7

August, 1991: In protest of US immigration policies, Harvard University announces that the Eighth International Conference on AIDS will be moved from Boston to Amsterdam.

November 1991: Magic Johnson announces he has HIV.

At the **end of 1991**, 257,750 are diagnosed with AIDS in the U.S., and 157,637 are dead from the disease.

In 1992, after years of pressure, the CDC expands the definition of AIDS to include: Cervical cancer, recurrent bacterial pneumonia, TB in the lungs, and fewer than 200 T-cells. The subsequent year, the number of women diagnosed with AIDS increases dramatically.

In 1993, in response to protests by ACT UP's Lesbian Caucus and others, HHS Secretary Donna Shalala forms a Lesbian AIDS Task Force. In subsequent months, the CDC begins funding lesbian-specific prevention programs, and the women's natural history study includes lesbians.

September 21

I didn't even finish typing in the date and I heard Stephan calling me from the bedroom. Maybe I'll have time tomorrow to write.

September 22

Yesterday was the day that wouldn't end. After four hours of sleep, I dragged my ass out of bed to get Stephan to the hospital so he could have the port put in his chest in order to make IV treatments easier. It took more than five hours. I read for a while and fell asleep (kind of) in the waiting room. Not fun.

We got home a little after three, both of us completely exhausted. I helped Stephan into bed, called his sister and mother and then took the phone off the hook and collapsed next to him.

I don't know how much rest I got before I woke up to Stephan moaning and rocking back and forth. His side was beginning to hurt him really badly. When I called the doctor, he suggested coming to the hospital, but Stephan refused. So we have an appointment for this morning at ten. Stephan took two nice dumps today (always cause for celebration), so whatever is going on, it's not interfering with his digestion.

The doctor took a look at him and thinks it may be related to the spleen. Stephan has to go back to the hospital again tomorrow for a CAT scan. And…there is a transfusion scheduled for the next day at 8:30.

Fortunately, someone else is on duty to bring Stephan to and from the hospital the next two days. It all feels endless and I could use time away from all this.

I took a little walk today, since Stephan's mom was over for her weekly visit. I found a sunny spot and fell asleep for a while in Washington Square Park. It was breezy and a little warm and felt soooooo good. I just lay down on the grass, closed my eyes, and let everything go.

The stress has been unbelievable the past few days. With each new problem, I feel a little hope and a little fear bubbling around in my heart. Hopeful the end is near (and always incredibly guilty for thinking that way), but so afraid of how it will play out and the pain that's in store for both of us.

September 24

Today, I found myself in bed, arms wrapped around my pillow, crying those paralyzing, gut wrenching tears. Fortunately, Stephan was at the hospital getting his transfusion, and I was able to really let go. I could hear myself asking "Why?" over and over, and then, "It hurts!" which sent me into even deeper, more convulsive sobs. Bigger moans, heavier sobs. Finally, after who knows how long, I lay on my bed completely exhausted.

Now my head feels about twice its normal size and I'm moving through this thick fog. Sadness weighs an awful lot.

The doctor is supposed to call this morning with the results from the CAT scan. I hold this secret hope we'll be told to start getting ready for the end; I don't think any of us needs another continuation. Not that I know how to help him get ready. And today, anyway, Stephan seems more willing to fight what is happening.

September 26

Last night, Stephan said he is finally coming to accept that he has a terminal disease. He talked about everything that happened this week, all the tests, the results of the CAT scan (he's got some kind of nodes in his stomach, and his spleen is inflamed). Without shame or hesitation, he cried and said he had nothing left to hope for. "It's only going to get worse. There's nothing I can do. I just want my old life back."

Suddenly, there are things he still wants to do, places he wants to go. Then, he looked at me and talked about how much our relationship had changed. "I don't know how to be with you. I don't even know who I am by myself!" I've been so distracted by my own emotional roller coaster, I forgot how much Stephan has to deal with.

One of Stephan's favorite sayings is, "Letting go is a receptive process." Stephan has a lot to let go of, and he knows very little of what else is to come. I have some letting go to do as well – mostly I have to let go of looking at the future and try to be a little more about the here and now. This thought scares me.

I just checked on Stephan. He's finally found a comfortable position after several nights of restless sleep. He is lying across the top of the bed with a pillow propped under his chin and another resting along his side. He's got a sniffle now and his chest sounds congested.

What he doesn't need right now is another infection, but he thinks he's got one. He said he had a hard time today. When I called from work, he was whispering and his breath was heavy.

I'm glad he's finally getting rest. I am in the living room reading and smoking. I've increased my smoking to almost a half a pack a day – most of it smoked at work. This is not good, I know, but I can't help myself. I'll stop again, just not today.

I've started reading without any music on. I have to now. I need the quiet in case Stephan calls. Every unfamiliar sound catches my attention. More than once, I thought Stephan was moaning, or calling my name. I'd look up, holding my breath, sitting perfectly still and listening… waiting. The quiet mocks me, and I go back to reading.

I did just check on him again. He was sound asleep. He must have been sweating because he wrapped a towel around his head like a turban.

October 6

Stephan fell into the bathtub last night while trying to sit down on the toilet. I was in the bedroom reading when I heard a loud CRASH! In the few seconds it took me to run into the bathroom, a thousand images went through my head. It felt like my life had stopped. I didn't know what I'd see. Was he unconscious? Dead?

Luckily, Stephan wasn't hurt, just scared. I helped him onto the toilet and washed his face. He looked confused. "I don't know what happened. I lost my balance and couldn't keep myself from falling." That shocked innocence is always unnerving to me; he becomes so helpless. It might be time to get a portable urinal for him to use in the bedroom.

October 9

Since Stephan's fall the other day, I've rearranged my work schedule. I work the next few days in a row, so Stephan is staying with his sister. I have to say: I feel an incredible sense of freedom without him around. I miss him and think about him, but I like not being the only one taking care of him. I like walking through the apartment without worrying if I'm making too much noise, or hearing my name called from the bedroom. It is incredibly draining.

It's not like I've done a whole lot with my free time – mostly I go to work, come home, and rest. Sometimes, it is hard to know what to do with myself. I'm not used to being with just me. I got the movie Grand Canyon from the video store, but I feel too restless to sit and watch it.

My plan was to start working another story that's been brewing in my head, but it is hard to get started.

With a little quiet time, I've let myself start to really think about my life and how it will look when Stephan is gone. Where will I live? Should I go back to counseling?

With everything we've been going through, I sometimes think I want to work with AIDS patients. Other times, I think that's the last thing I should be doing.

Then, there are always the fantasies about running away. They come up a lot. California, New Mexico. Anywhere but here. It's nice to disappear into another world, another life. It all seems perfect there.

October 12

"I'm trying. I'm trying." I had another one of my crying spells. It started out as an attempt at meditating, but the next thing I knew, I was sobbing uncontrollably. I couldn't stop. I kept rocking back and forth, moaning, "I'm trying," in a voice I didn't recognize. I am less afraid of these meltdowns than I used to be. It's odd to become so familiar with pain. It still rattles me and holds me, but now, I know it won't last.

And there's always the sweetest sleep that follows where I float above and away from my life for a while. Stephan came home from his sister's yesterday. He wasn't even through the door when he started. "Can we close the window? Why is it so cold? I think I'm thirsty…"

Whatever calm I had while he was gone disappeared in a heartbeat. I found out later that he had taken medication and was a little high from it, but it felt like I had just opened the door on a whirlwind. It was all I could do not to start crying again.

Today his mood and behavior were a little better – at least, he wasn't as demanding. Even though no one was with Stephan, I left at ten to do my volunteer work for the AIDS Walk. It's really become my only opportunity to connect with other people and be in a world that isn't demanding of me. Stephan said he'd be fine and promised not to get up unless he absolutely had to. I worried about him nonstop. When I called, he said he got up and made it to the bathroom and the couch without any problem. He's a stubborn bastard.

Stephan said his family wants to have a meeting to talk about the what/how/who of taking care of him. I'm not sure what to say. It is clear that he and I can't manage without help, and I know his family has their own individual lives to live. Stephan wants to stay home; I'm not sure how much longer that's possible.

It's funny: When he's feeling OK, we spend time together, and I am ready to take on whatever comes our way. I feel my love for him and I want to help him, take care of him. But when things are hard and he's not doing well, I don't see how it is possible to keep on, without losing everything we have financially and emotionally. I never thought I'd be in a position where I'd have to find some hospice care for Stephan. I hate even thinking about it.

He lays in the bedroom tired, holding on for reasons I don't even think he understands, and I'm out here plotting ways to send him away. I feel awful. I am confused. I don't know what to do or how to do anything. On Wednesday, he goes back over to his sister's house, and I work through until Sunday. Our lives have become a big checkers game, moving from square to square, trying not to get jumped.

October 15

Mom called yesterday. She wanted to see how I was and to let me know she and Dad were thinking about me. When she asked how I was, I said, "Okay," in a monotone voice. I wasn't up for playing nice. "Just okay?" she asked, sounding curious (or confused). Did I really have to explain to her why I wasn't in a good mood? We had a weird, strained conversation, as usual. I talked about my writing a little bit and my job even less. I did not mention Stephan at all.

There is little that changes. This phone call becomes one of our empty conversations that connect us – same song, different verse, neither of us fluent in the other's language of life.

She'll never know about the times when I get so overwhelmed and don't have any strength. Or when I get angry and resent what Stephan is "doing" to me. I don't tell her how awful it feels when I can't find the beauty of living anywhere.

I creep along from day to day, my family ignorant to the struggle Stephan and I are facing. We're in this horrible battle, and, we're losing.

I miss that sense of security and my ability to know where I stand. I have no idea what is keeping me going, except that I know I have to.

When friends call and ask what they can do for me, I don't have an answer. I don't know what anyone can do for me. I don't know what to do myself. I am completely fucking miserable, period. What can anyone do about that? Nothing can change. Stephan continues to hang on, and I hate him for that. I want to yell at him and ask him what the point is. What's he trying to do? Why won't he just give up – or give in?

October 23

Yesterday, Stephan's mom was here for "her day." These days are pretty hard for him. He hates being taken care of and worries about how his disease is affecting her. Before I left, I told him to stop being so stubborn and guilty and let his mother take care of him. It's what she wants to do.

When I got home last night, we sat on the couch and he told me about his day and what his mom did for him. I want to try my best to use his words:

"I wasn't feeling good and I just lay here most of the day. My mom fixed me lunch, but all I could eat was soup. She wanted to feed it to me, it seemed important to her, so I let her." His lip quivered and tears started rolling down his face. "When I finished eating, she said to just rest for a while.

We hardly spoke all day, and that was okay. I fell asleep and she sat in the chair crocheting. Sometimes I'd wake up and look at her. We'd both just kind of smile a little. It felt like when you were a kid and you weren't feeling good and your mother says everything's going to be all right – and you believed her.

"At one point, I opened my eyes. She was sitting there with her eyes closed, resting. There is no conflict in her. None. She does what she needs to, without question, and has her faith to help her through the hard times. She helped me relax today. I haven't felt that way in a long time."

We both sat on the couch, holding hands and crying. I love Miss Betty. She really is not one to question what she's been given. I can't imagine what it must feel like to see your son wasting away right in front of you, yet she just comes in every week with her sweet potato pie and fried chicken and does what she can.

I have never had any long, deep conversation with her. In fact, I hardly know her at all, except what I see in the few hours she is here each week. She is truly a graceful, giving woman. We are lucky she is here for us.

When I brought him to bed, Stephan told me again how much he loved me and how thankful he was that I was in his life. He said I taught him about love and how to grow in a relationship. He said he wanted me to go on and do everything I wanted to, or at least try because that's what he had done and he had no regrets. He also said he was ready to go and didn't think it would be long. He wasn't afraid of death, but he said the permanence of it scared him. I told him it scares me, too.

Then we talked about all the things we had done together (our trip to Cancun and the Mayan ruins, my birthday surprise in New York, the Apollo Theater, the dance company...) and for those few moments, we weren't afraid. It was peaceful, complete, loving. All the tension and worry I felt faded, and Stephan and I were together.

When I came to bed later, he held me close to him, and I let myself believe everything was like it used to be. Safe, warm, and full of promise.

October 25

Stephan's been having a lot of dreams where he is being chased. They frighten him so much that he is afraid to go to sleep. This morning we talked about what's been happening with him physically. His doctor wants to put him in the hospital tomorrow and run another CAT scan and get a better idea of what's going on. Stephan agreed, but only if his stay is as short as possible. Once again, we will be dealing with visiting hours and tests and the fallout Stephan feels from being in the hospital.

I tried to tell Stephan he has a choice in how this works out. He can decide what tests he wants and what medication he will take. He's pretty confused and very afraid. I told him it was all right to be afraid, that, in fact, he should be. I also said it was possible to be other things at the same time. He could be love, he could allow himself to find safety and comfort in the love he felt for his family and me. This is where he could find peace, like the other day when his Mom was here.

I heard myself talking to him about death and the fact that he couldn't hide from it. None of us could. No matter what medicine he took, or what tests were done, he was going to die, most likely before me. We sat on the couch, and I held him like a little boy, and we cried. "I'm afraid," he kept saying. "I don't want it to hurt."

A year ago, we were getting ready for "Slaves to the Rhythm," the biggest, most successful production of Stephan's career. Now that seems like light years away, and so simple compared to what we're in the middle of.

October 26

We planned to go to the AIDS Walk yesterday, but it was too cold. So we went over to a friend's house for dinner instead. Stephan couldn't make it up the four flights of stairs, so he was carried. Not that Stephan didn't try. But after two flights, he was pretty winded and didn't protest when one of our friends came right up behind him and picked him up, carrying him up the next two flights, two steps at a time. I know Stephan was embarrassed; he kept saying he didn't know he was so weak. Aside from that, it was a fun night, and Stephan got a chance to see a few friends he hadn't seen in a while. When we got home, though, we both went straight to bed.

Today started out looking pretty good. His doctor decided it wasn't necessary for Stephan to go into the hospital, and he seemed to be feeling okay. At least as okay as one can feel in his situation. A CAT scan was going to be scheduled, and it was discovered one of Stephan's medications was probably the cause for his nightmares.

From there, though, it got a little confusing. First, Stephan was going to have the CAT scan. Then we talked about what the point would be in having it done, since we were both clear that he wasn't going to take any more medication, so the CAT scan was canceled. Once that was settled, he tried to eat some lunch but didn't get three forkfuls in before he was in the bathroom with an upset stomach and the runs. I guess he got a little scared, because when I got back from the bank, he was waiting to hear from the doctor's office about when he would be scheduled for the test.

We talked more about what our plans were. He wanted to find out why he was having a hard time eating. He was also clear that he would not take any more medication. It was a hard, realistic conversation – another step down the ladder to wherever it is we're going.

When the doctor called, Stephan asked about the CAT scan and what would happen if he found anything. Chemotherapy. Stephan heard this and made himself very clear: He would NOT have the procedure. In fact, he would continue taking whatever medicines he had now, but he was not interested in any other treatments. He would keep his regular appointments, but going forward, he wanted only to be kept comfortable.

When Stephan hung up the phone, he looked at me and smiled and said, "Well, we've done it."

KEY WEST

Six years passed between the time I dropped out of my student teaching and began graduate school. During that time, my visits home felt strained and hopeful at the same time. I knew that I confused my parents, and I understood their worry. I was confused, too. They were right: dropping out didn't make sense. Just waiting tables was the epitome of not living up to my potential.

Meanwhile, my interactions with my siblings were easier, even though I still felt guarded around them. Most of my siblings were in the marriage phase of life, which made our interactions easier, mostly because there was more distance.

When I did visit my family, babies and toddlers kept us distracted, and it almost felt like being together was easy. And, for the most, part it was easy, except that I'd sit in the middle of it all, wondering how it would change when I finally told everyone I was gay.

We were nineteen when Tim, my twin brother, came out to me – just before he moved to San Francisco, where he would continue his dance and theater training. I remember listening to him talk and making this very clear decision not to say anything about the sexual confusion that I was experiencing. First of all, I still considered my occasional gay hookups an experiment — I was still dating women, wasn't I? Second, I knew Tim well enough to keep whatever gay leanings I had to myself. This was his moment. For me to reveal that there was another aspect of our lives where we were similar would not sit well with him. And I was right. Years later, when I finally came out to him, he said, "There's a part of me that feels upset – it's one more thing that's not my own."

It was with the help of therapy that my gay life expanded beyond the anonymous grope at a bookstore to the occasional drink at one of the gay clubs in town. My favorite was a place called Key West, off Thirteenth St. It had a three-story waterfall on one wall and a dance floor that was dark and crowded on Friday nights.

Every time I walked into the club, I was walking into a new, exciting, nerve-wracking world. I was constantly worried that I'd run into someone I knew. Most nights, I'd grab a drink and then stand in the shadows watching, waiting. If I got up the nerve to talk with someone, I used a fake name. I liked Derrick. I thought the name had a sense of mystery to it.

When I bought my first gay newspaper from a newsstand, my hands were literally shaking; I was waiting for everyone walking by to scream and point at me. It's odd now to look back and remember that pointless shame – ten years of wasted time and energy. Still, I was making progress.

When I met Finn, my first boyfriend, it was a giant step forward in accepting my gay identity. He was tall, masculine, sexy, and came right up to me one night at Key West and asked if I wanted to dance. In a heartbeat, I went from insecure wallflower to prom queen. As we moved around the dance floor, Finn kept telling me how hot I was and leaned his pretty face in to give me long, sensual kisses.

Finn, it turns out, was a dancer and a nursing student at Community College of Philadelphia on Spring Garden Street. It was a hot and heavy romance from that first night. We would meet up after classes for lunch or dinner. A few times, I stayed over at his place in New Jersey. It was my first experience sleeping next to someone who snored – loudly.

Fortunately, Finn redeemed himself with his incredible sexual appetite. We had a lot of fun. I also found someone I could talk with about all the pain and struggle I'd been going through. He didn't have any answers for me about how to solve the conflict with my family, but Finn understood.

How nice it was, to be completely understood.

One of the best things to come from my relationship with Finn was the group of friends he introduced me to. I would sit among this group of out, proud, strong, funny gay men and drink it in. I wanted those afternoons to go on forever. Finn and his friends made it all seem so easy. And when I was with them, it was easy. It was life with no apologies.

When Finn began pulling away, I thought my world was going to implode. To lose the relationship was one thing, but the friends I had met? What was I going to do? I was so afraid I'd be stuck back at zero, alone again, struggling to find a place and people to laugh with. I called his friend Stephan in a panic, and the minute I heard him say hello in that sandy, silky voice of his, I knew things were going to be okay.

The first time I met Stephan Love was after a dance class that he and Finn were taking. Finn and I made plans to meet for lunch. I showed up early and stood by the door watching as Finn moved across the floor, working the combination, completely drenched in sweat. Next to him was a man with light brown skin who moved so easily, like he was gliding.

He had eyes that somehow looked both amused and unyielding. I couldn't stop watching him. This man, it turned out, was Stephan, and he was joining us for lunch. Stephan had a distracting way about him—I'd never seen such confidence and effortless grace in a man. And he was masculine at the same time. He moved like a cat. Then there was his voice! That sexy, deep voice. He could have worked in radio.

We sat at a hoagie shop waiting for our sandwiches when Stephan noticed one of the people from dance class enter the shop, order a sandwich, and take a table by himself. I recognized the guy immediately—he was a little older, not very coordinated, and stood by himself. "I'm going to see if Carl wants to join us. I'll be right back," Stephan said to us, and walked over to where this guy sat alone.

I remember watching him walk away and thinking, Who IS this guy? Two weeks later, the three of us met up for Halloween at a club called Kurt's. I thought I was being clever when I showed up in a T-shirt that said, "This IS my Halloween costume." Finn decided to dress like he had just come out of the shower wearing a towel around his waste and soap on a rope around his neck. He looked hot. We were pushing our way through the crowd, trying to find Stephan, when Finn pointed up to one of the speakers and said, "There he is."

Stephan was dancing on one of the speaker boxes with a drag queen with a huge blond wig. His costume was like nothing I had ever seen. He was dressed as a "Flasher' only, when he opened his coat, he revealed a flesh-colored body suit with an incredibly huge set of genitalia. He used tube socks to shape the penis and balls, and brown yarn for this tangled mess of pubic hair. It was absolutely obscene. And hilarious.

There was a crowd around the speaker cheering Stephan and the drag queen on. I watched him up there, and for the second time, I wondered, Who IS this guy?

A few weeks later, when I was visiting my parents, Mom placed a newspaper article in front of me and said, "I saved this for you, thought you might like it. It's about this guy who's doing work with kids using dance."
There on the front page of the Metro section was a half-page picture of Stephan in a dance studio, sitting against the mirror, smiling and looking away from the camera. The headline read, "Gotta Dance, Gotta Teach," and an article followed. Here is a brief excerpt:

...Stephan Love incorporated social issues into his dance lessons, and then went on the road with his company performing shows full of dance and energy that also focused on the problems of society. "It started out with them coming to me with their personal problems and things that were happening to their friends," Love, 32, said of his students. ''Then I just felt like something more could be done, not just for them but for other children and teenagers as well." Love's dance ensemble is called the Next Generation Performance Group: 18 youngsters, ranging in age from 8 to 17, whose budding skills are supplemented with lessons and rap sessions on the sometimes harsh realities of life.

It is entertainment with a message, a way to face controversial topics through drama, said Love, a choreographer, dancer and producer who has appeared in television, on videos and on stage.

Stephan Love is the kind of instructor who accompanies his wards, many of whom travel some distance to get to his studio, from the school to the subway. Other students, who come from the suburbs and New Jersey, are safely placed on the train with a goodbye hug.

"Their parents place them in my care. I have to take care of them," Love said.

Love, a man with piercing brown eyes and a ready smile, does indeed confess that his young wards help him feel younger: "I'm the first person to say that I'm definitely suffering from the Peter Pan syndrome." When it comes to his lessons, Peter Pan can quickly turn into Capt. Hook, the students say. Love's students are required to write essays on social issues, take written tests and receive video critiques. They must choreograph their own dance routine, and they are expected to be able to perform in commercials and television shows as well as on stage.

Currently, the students are taping a dance video dealing with child abuse, for distribution to schools nationwide.

I sat at the kitchen table reading the article with my heart pounding in my ears; sweat suddenly dripping down my back. I couldn't tell my mother that I knew Stephan, who knew what can of worms that would have opened. I was trying to be nonchalant, anxious she would see something in my face that revealed this – and other – deeper secrets. At the same time, I was thrilled for Stephan and wanted to call him right away.

He was everything I hoped to be: successful, respected, talented, caring... and out. Later on, as I got ready to leave, I grabbed the paper and said, "Mind if I take this with me? Maybe I can interview this guy for one of my classes."

Mom nodded, saying, "I thought you'd like that. He's doing some good work."

AIDS Timeline #8

By <u>June 1993</u>, sexual transmission passes injection drug use as the major form of HIV transmission for women.

The US Postal Service issues a commemorative AIDS Awareness red ribbon stamp, <u>Spring 1993</u>.

At the <u>end of 1993</u>: 411,887 are diagnosed with AIDS in the US, and 241,787 are dead.

By <u>1995</u>, the "AIDS cocktail," also called HAART (Highly Active Anti-Retroviral Therapy) is developed. A multi-drug approach to treating HIV, this medication breakthrough changes the tide of the epidemic, and people begin talking about living with HIV, not dying from AIDS.

<u>August, 1996</u>, The Committee of Ten-Thousand, a group of Hemophiliacs who were infected by tainted blood products, files a federal class-action lawsuit against the companies that make clotting factor.

October 28

Someone suggested that pot might help with Stephan's stomach pain. Given his pneumonia history, there's no way he can smoke it, so I learned how to make pot butter from Stephan's brother in law. The THC somehow transfers into the butter and then we can spread a little on a cracker or something. Hopefully this will help Stephan eat without becoming nauseous. Pot has been sitting in melted butter in the double boiler for a while now and should be finished soon.

All I can say is, our apartment REEKS! I hope none of the neighbors can smell it.

An old friend of Stephan's is in from out of town and called, wanting to stop by. Stephan heard me casually say today might not be a good day and suggested he check in tomorrow. Stephan asked why I minimize our situation with people, and I said I wasn't sure how much he wanted anyone to know, and actually, I didn't see things as that bad.

The truth was, I said, I expected them to get worse. This was not what Stephan wanted to hear. "Maybe this is as bad as it will get. Maybe I've suffered enough, and I won't get any worse. I don't want to hear what you think might will happen! You don't really know!"

I left him in the bedroom and tried to fix my lunch. I felt hollow, so sad. I could feel the rumble of tears grow from the pit of my stomach, and I gave into them. Suddenly, I found myself on the floor of the kitchen, holding my knees and rocking back and forth. My body shook with sobs, over and over I heard myself saying, "It hurts, it hurts."

I don't know how long this went on, but soon, my tears became more of a prayer – asking for relief. The more I prayed, the heavier my crying became. I felt like I was suspended above myself, looking down at a broken man crying like a five-year-old. How does anyone find comfort from so much pain?

The tears stopped like they always do. My stomach hurt and I lost my appetite. I fixed my lunch, anyway, and I made myself eat and surprised myself by eating everything. Now, I just feel relief.

The tears are still there. I feel them all the time; a silent undercurrent constantly pulls at my heart. I still don't have any answers about how long, and I can no longer run away from the fact that I was given the strength to deal with what is happening, despite how hard I try.

October 30

I was sitting in the living room, paying bills and trying not to get too worried about what little money we have when I heard Stephan call from the bedroom. "Hon?" There's always the slightest sound of confusion in his voice when he calls, like he's not sure where he is or if I am really here. He says sometimes he gets caught in his dreams and they follow him when he wakes up.

When I walked into the bedroom, he was leaning on his elbow looking at the bed sheets. There was a huge puddle of sweat under him and his face was dripping. "I'm wet."

I brought him some towels, dried him off, and covered the pillow and sheets. He lay back down and asked why he was sweating so much.

This is his latest thing, to try and find out why things are happening, as if somehow once he found out, he could fix it. He's now using a "patch" for his pain medicine, and usually, when a patch is changed, he does sweat a little more than usual. I offered this as an explanation, which he seemed to accept.

Yesterday, he decided to sit on the couch and eat something. He was trying to figure out when and why he started to feel so bad this time around. I knew. His health and mood took a dive after he heard about one of his old friends dying. He cried for such a long time and retreated into himself, seeming to give up a little.

When I said this to him, he stared out the window and started to cry again. "You're right," he said through little sobs. "I didn't think it would affect me like this. I loved him… and I never told him. I never got the chance to say that. It's my own fault."

We talked about how Stephan could still say goodbye. Maybe he could write a letter, or we could have a ceremony of some kind. Stephan liked the idea of a letter and said he would write one. I can't imagine what it feels like to bump blindly into death while looking at your own physical decline.

Once again, there is little that I can do except offer my own insights and interpretations and hope it helps. Yesterday, it felt okay to be Stephan's support. I held him and talked with him. It felt good as he put his head on my lap and said he was a lucky man to have me in his life. In that moment, I felt the same way about him.

Today? Today my head feels like it is being squeezed by vice grips and there's a twitch in my left eye. I look at myself in the mirror and see wrinkles and circles under my eyes. This past year has taken its toll on me. I feel drained, completely empty. Fortunately, Stephan is going to his sister's house tonight and won't be back until Monday.

It's weird: as much as I welcome this time, it also reminds me of how alone I feel, and soon will be.

Our experiment with the pot and butter seems to have its good and bad points. It definitely settles his stomach, but it also makes him sleepy. I actually like it and have had more than a few crackers of my own. With Stephan, we'll have to play with how much we use until we can find something that helps without putting Stephan in a fog for hours – he doesn't need any help with that.

October 31

Everything changes when Stephan is not here. I felt it when I came home from work last night. There's an emptiness that feels both soothing and frightening. I am not used to it. A part of me feels that I have to absorb it as quickly as possible, before it disappears. Maybe Stephan will come home early, maybe he'll suddenly get sick. My tense silence would be snatched from me before I even had a chance to embrace it.

So, I am pretending that I like it. I am trying to convince myself that I am happy to have these few hours of solitude. Isn't this how I can take care of myself?

There is so much I could do before Stephan's return on Monday. There's The Ritz Movie Theater with the best popcorn in the city, only a few blocks away. I could read, sleep, and walk aimlessly through town. I could even go spend a few hours at Border's and eat out by myself like I see so many people do at restaurants.

These choices all involve getting up, getting out, and I don't feel quite up to showering and making myself look human. It would be nice to spend time with a friend or two, but I find myself struggling to find a friend I could call. There are a few, I know. But the truth is, if I were to call, I'd end up talking about Stephan, and I would get weepy and sad.

I know they love me and want to help, but the sympathetic looks remind me that we're all helpless in this. I'm not in the mood for that.

I've already written a little. I've got a story brewing right now. Unfortunately, it feels too new. After a few attempts, I've already closed that file. Now, I am even struggling for something to write here. I guess it's time to find something else to distract me for a while.

November 4

There is little to write about. Everything is the same. Stephan came home from his sister's Monday afternoon and my time alone ended. All I did was sleep and watch

TV while he was away. That's it. I tried to write but couldn't. I went out for a while, but it wasn't fun by myself.

Life seems to be moving me along, and for the moment it is relatively painless. I guess I should be thankful for the reprieve, but I know this calm never lasts, so I'm trying to stay in this moment and not think about what might happen.

I spoke with Mom and Dad the other night. I made the mistake of asking Dad what he thought about the election. He gave me quite an earful, and I found myself half-listening to what he said. I wasn't interested in any discussion with him about politics. Mom asked me what my plans were for Thanksgiving. Who knows? They also invited me up to the house "for a break from everything." I might go visit next weekend. I'll have to wait and see if I've got enough in me to play the game.

November 5

Stephan must be sleeping 15 to 18 hours a day. "Is something wrong?" he asks me in this whispered, groggy voice. "No, baby," I say. "Just rest if you want to, your body must need it." Then he settles himself into the pillow and rests his head on my hand. "I trust you. Everything is all right," he sighs, and I stroke his head.

I check on him every hour or so. He looks so small under the quilts. I see the steady rise and fall of his breathing, and I hope his dreams are peaceful. He has grown more and more childlike. There is innocence to his voice, a reassurance he seems to be looking for that is both endearing and sad.

Sometimes I hear him call for his mother in his sleep. When I go over and touch his cheek, his eyes open with a start and then they close slowly with an exhausted breath. This morning, he didn't want to be by himself. "I need to feel safe," he half-mumbled as he put his head in my lap. "You are," I said and tried to soothe him. "You are."

We sat like that in bed for so long that my legs went completely numb. Still I sat, watching the traffic along the Ben Franklin Bridge, imagining us somewhere above everything, and for a few moments, we WERE safe. I could feel a rush of love fill me, and I smiled and kissed Stephan's shoulder.

We have a doctor appointment this afternoon, just a monthly check-in. I don't expect anything to change dramatically in terms of what we are doing now. We've hit another plateau, a little time for all of us to catch our breath.

November 8

One year ago today, it was opening night for Slaves to the Rhythm, our most elaborate, most successful production we had ever staged, involving a cast of 20, soundtrack recording and building an enormous pyramid shaped set. It got great reviews, and firmly established Stephan and the dance company in the Philadelphia dance scene. Slaves would also be the last time the company ever performed together. Stephan and I were running around, crazily taking care of last minute details. We were terribly excited, completely exhausted. The show was finally a reality.

What a difference a year makes. I don't know what else to say about it. So much has changed, too much. When I think over what has happened, it's hard to believe what we've gone through. Now our days are measured by what Stephan eats, how he sleeps, who will watch him while I'm at work.

Time seems to pass slowly, one day dripping into another. I do my best to parcel out my time so that don't get too burned out and can take care of myself – a concept I still don't completely understand. I haven't felt like writing much in my journal – little to say, though I see subtle changes, which I'm sure will become more obvious in time.

Stephan rarely gets out of bed now. When he does, it is only to use the bathroom. It's becoming more and more difficult for him stand for long periods of time without his knees buckling. He is like a newborn colt trying to figure out how to use his legs. Soon, I won't be able to support him while we shower.

He's also starting to develop this childlike way of asking for things. Like a five-year-old, he makes his wishes known. "I have to eat before 7:00," he said the other evening. When I asked why, he shrugged and said, "Just because." Another time, he woke me up at six A.M., nudging my shoulder and saying, "I'm hungry, when are we having breakfast?"

There is no anger in his voice, no frustration, just a simple need that must be satisfied, as soon as possible. I pulled myself together and stumble into the kitchen to make his breakfast. We have been going along like this for so long, it has just become second nature.

November 9

It was another long, difficult day for Stephan and me. Stephan overheard a conversation I was having on the phone. He said, "I heard you say it was your day off today. It really isn't. I can't remember when you had a day off. I can't remember when I had a day off. It feels like this just goes on forever." And so it does.

I can feel the tide of emotion swelling inside me again. I guess I'm due for a good cry. The other day I talked with a friend who asked, "Isn't anyone there to comfort you?" There was a curiosity in his voice, a wonder of how I manage by myself. I shrugged off his question and changed the subject.

My tears are private, like my pain. I have no problem sharing how tired I am or worried I feel, but my tears? They are my own. There's no way to call someone for help when you're buried under pain and can't find your way out. I barely know where I am, let alone know how to dial a friend. And the pain? There aren't any words for it. I can't describe it. And I'm too busy trying to survive it. I'm learning all the time that it never lasts. Like everything else, it changes.

For now, my energy is centered on helping Stephan and getting through each day. We spend a lot of time in the bedroom, his head on my shoulders. Stephan's latest kick is apples and peanut butter. I peel and slice apples for him, putting a little dab of peanut butter on each piece. When he drinks his juice, he takes his straw and slurps up the juice nearest the top, where the ice has melted. He says it is colder there and feels good going down his throat. I am amused by these little habits he's adopted and make sure there is plenty of ice in his juice.

November 13

Neuropathy. The newest word added to our medical vocabulary. This is apparently what is making Stephan's feet sensitive. The other night, just having the bed sheet against his toes created an unbelievable wave of pain through his feet. It has something to do with the nervous system. We got a prescription for Elavil, which is supposed to help relieve the pain. Stephan is also supposed to get his feet rubbed three times a day to help with circulation. After breakfast this morning, I rubbed his feet as gently as I could. He winced and grimaced all the way through but said he felt better afterwards. I guess it helps.

After a horrible night, Stephan lay around this morning trying to rest but was having a difficult time doing so. He was sweating all night and more this morning. I have changed the towels and his shirt three times in the last few hours. For a while, I sat in the bedroom reading and watching him. I kept sending him calming thoughts of peace and love. I even believed it worked because occasionally I'd see him take a deep breath and close his eyes.

Those quiet moments were interrupted by endless minutes of his staring into the middle of nowhere. I asked what he thought about when he was so far away. He said he thinks about his mother. Then he quickly followed with, "I have this cough again. And I'm bringing up a lot of mucous." His lips were chapped and sweat ran down his temples. "I'm having a hard time breathing and I'm so tired. I didn't get any sleep last night."

Tired as he was, his body still tried to push on. In the middle of a sentence, he said he needed the bathroom, and FAST! I tried to move him as fast as I could, half dragging his feet as we shuffled to the bathroom.

Unfortunately we were not fast enough and his bowels let go just before I got him on the toilet. He fell to his knees, breathing heavy and looking defeated. "Look at my underwear, they're a mess!" I didn't reply. Instead, I filled the sink and grabbed a washcloth, trying not to let him see my tears. When he was ready, we made our way back to the bedroom and he collapsed onto the bed. As I washed off his legs and bottom, he quietly cried.

"Every day it's something different," he sobbed. "It doesn't stop."

We talked often about when he would die, and the reasons why he might still be here. As he cried, I realized that part of his struggle might be that he doesn't know how to stop living. His whole life had been one of survival. Accepting the passing of life —that's a whole different thing. I talked with him about how hard he worked his whole life, especially these past few months.

"It's okay to rest," I said. "You don't have to try so hard now. Just relax. It's okay." It took time, but eventually, Stephan closed his eyes and fell asleep.

November 14

I went to the movies last night for the first time in I don't know how long. One of our friends stayed with Stephan, and I jumped at the chance to get away for a while. Yesterday was really hard for me. Stephan shitting himself left me completely drained all day. The chance to be distracted by a movie was exactly what I needed. I wish it lasted longer.

I barely got my coat off and Stephan was asking for some cold water. Just like that, he smacked me back into the middle of my life. Sleep came easily for both of us, and I woke this morning feeling better than I had in a while. After a very light breakfast of watermelon, Stephan wanted to sleep more. He's wrapped himself up like a baby, tucked under the quilts and blanket. His eyes were big as saucers, and he looked completely helpless. We both think he is fighting some kind of cold or pneumonia again. His voice is hoarse and high pitched, and his cough is more noticeable.

When we talked about his cough this morning, Stephan said he didn't want another fifteen days of Pentam treatment. He doesn't want any more drug treatments, period. If it is true, and the pneumonia is back, he just wants to be kept comfortable.

I asked him how he felt about this. "There is nothing else to do," he said quietly. I know my job is to help him remember what he said about no more treatments. I wish I knew what those words really meant. Lately, Stephan has talked about seeing other people in the apartment. Maybe spirit guides were making themselves known to him.

Maybe they were there for support. If this were true, I should be encouraging him to talk to these "people." I wonder if I should try talking to them myself. Maybe all of this is bullshit – who knows? It can't hurt to try. The worse that will come out of it is nothing, and we've already got that.

November 19

Where to start? Where to start? Stephan had blood drawn the other day. His hemoglobin is dangerously low. The nurse called yesterday morning and said he needed an emergency transfusion. She was going to call the doctor and arrange to have it done ASAP. This will be his fourth transfusion. Each time, he has been sicker afterwards. In fact, after the last one, Stephan said he would not get another.

Once again, he sang a different song when faced with the decision. I asked if he was sure he wanted to go through with the transfusion. It wouldn't make much of a difference in the long run. I tried to talk to him about the process of acceptance and letting go. Stephan was not too receptive. He got angry and told me I had no idea what he was going through. He said, "I'm scared to death. I feel like if I don't take the transfusion, then I'll be committing suicide. I can't do that. I want death to happen naturally."

When the doctor called, he made it clear what the consequences would be. "He can take the transfusion, or he can run the risk of his heart stopping at any time. There is not enough oxygen pumping through his body. If he doesn't take this, it is just a matter of time."

It all feels senseless. Stephan has become weak, so empty. He sleeps and eats and every so often, we talk for a few minutes. I know part of my reaction is my own selfishness. I can see it. I can also see how little Stephan has left. I know he's not happy. I know he wants to go. I don't know how to help him. I don't know how to reach him.

He's so frightened that all the conversations we've had about spirituality and the freedom found in death escape him now. My only choice is to accept what he has chosen and try to support him – and maybe even learn from it. If he is still here, his life is not over yet. There is still a lesson here – for both of us.

The nurse is in the bedroom and has begun the transfusion. Stephan is getting three pints of blood. This will take all day. I don't expect much to change. I don't know what Stephan expects; he hasn't talked to me about it. He just stares off into nowhere. My guess is that he's trying to make some sense of what this means and how to accept it. Maybe he'll find the answers, maybe he won't.

November 20

For almost nine hours, the nurse stayed here as the blood drained into Stephan's port. Today, we are dealing with the unpleasant side effects of the transfusion. Over all, they seem less difficult than the last time. The nurse says Stephan will be "feeling much better in a day or two." I'm not optimistic. I expect nothing to change. Stephan won't be able to get up by himself. He'll continue to have trouble getting dressed. He sure as hell won't be able to bathe himself. He may "feel better," but it's temporary.

It's funny: When I sat down to write, I wasn't feeling so angry. Yet now, I feel it pulsing in my head. My sister came for a visit today, and at one point asked if I was angry. I told her, "No. No. I don't feel angry. I get tired, and confused about why it has to happen, but I don't think I feel angry." I lied.

November 21

Morning has melted into afternoon without my having any sense of what time it is. I have written for about an hour, read for a while, bathed Stephan, talked with him for a bit, and watched TV. I'm also (thankfully) stoned. After I washed Stephan this afternoon, we brought the commode from the shower to the bedroom. It was the first time we tried this arrangement, and I felt awkward trying to make sure the water didn't soak the floor.

Somehow, we managed, and I dried him off quickly and brought him out to the living room. He hasn't been out there for over a week and was pleased with the change of scenery. I covered him with a bed sheet and two Afghan throws and asked, "Do you really believe in what we used to talk about when we first met—the idea that we have chosen certain lessons for this life?"

"Yeah," he sighed, "but I don't know how to use it now." He talked about how hard it was to accept what was happening to him. He wants to, but he doesn't know how. He feels confused and can't find a way to translate his beliefs into behavior.

"I don't know how." Stephan said, staring out the window. "I'm so afraid. I watch you moving around here. You've accepted what is happening. I don't know how. I feel like I have to keep going, I can't stop."

"You can," I said, stroking his head. I couldn't fight my tears, didn't want to. "I'm going to be okay. I love you so much."

"I know," Stephan said, closing his eyes. "But I don't want to leave you. I'm afraid of losing you." I wish I could describe how incredibly powerful this moment was. It was complete love. I hope Stephan felt this, too. It will help him.

I'M (FINALLY) COMING OUT

After Finn and I broke up, Stephan and I began to hang out a lot and quickly became close friends. I started working with him and the dance company, helping formulate how to address the issues Stephan thought kids should be talking about—drug abuse, peer pressure, child abuse, even AIDS.

His dance pieces, performed by this incredible dance group, were powerful, poignant. The fact that it was children dancing, and evoking such powerful responses from the audience, only added to the impact of the performances. The first time I saw the company perform, it was to Pat Benatar's "Hell is for Children." I couldn't take my eyes off the stage. It was absolutely riveting. The professional level of the dancing was one thing, but the emotion these kids brought to that piece was palpable. I was in tears by the time the piece ended. And the audience was on their feet.

My friendship with Stephan was nothing short of transformational. He always said, "I was born poor, black, and gay. I've got three strikes against me already. Doesn't matter a whole lot what I do or say, so why not do it big?" And he did. I was happy to ride in the wake of such confidence.

To think things could get any bigger (or better) was unimaginable. One night, Stephan and I were talking on the phone, and he said, "I am going to say something, and I don't want you to respond. I need you to just listen, and then think before you say anything. I am falling in love with you. I didn't plan it, wasn't expecting it, but that's it, plain and simple. I'm not expecting you to do anything. We don't have to let this change a thing about who we are as friends. I just wanted to be completely honest with you."

I was lying on the floor in the dining room, feet propped up on a chair, completely speechless. This guy was falling for me? I couldn't wrap my mind around that one – I remember saying something about appreciating his honesty and needing a little time to think about what he had said.

The next time we got together, it was a done deal. Before I got in the door we were making out. How could I say no to the one person in my world that was living his life so completely? I wanted any and all of whatever Stephan had to offer. I was scared to death of what it meant, but I was done waiting for something to happen.

When I completed my Master's Degree, Stephan took me to New York to celebrate. We stayed at the Waldorf Astoria, saw Into the Woods, and moved through the city liked we owned it. I was feeling more in charge of my life and excited about the future than I had ever felt. Not only did I have a relationship that I loved, I had found a job at Child Guidance Clinic, one of the most important institutions in children's and family therapy in the country. I was hired to help develop a newly funded "at risk" program for kids. My boss was a free spirited, funny, insightful woman who became one of my greatest teachers, Sandra. She encouraged me to follow my instincts and taught me what it meant to be a good therapist. The fact that I was a gay man meant as much to her as what color socks I wore.

It didn't take long for Sandra, my new supervisor, to become our new best friend. She adored Stephan. The three of us spent many nights at her home eating great food and telling endless stories. She would also become one of the most important people in our lives when Stephan's health grew worse.

I was far away from the judgments and the limited thinking that framed my childhood. As my therapist would say, I was "letting go of the shoulds" and finding my own voice.

There I was: a new job, a new relationship, and a new, exciting life and having brunch with my Dad. We talked about my work a bit, and eventually, he fell into his usual catch phrases about hard work, being honest, finding happiness. I knew he believed in these things. I also knew that when he started talking that way, he was saying he loved and believed in me.

As I listened to him, it occurred to me that I would never have an opportunity like this again. Sitting with my father, discussing my future and what it meant to be happy. I looked at him and said, "It's a little ironic you should be saying these things, because there's something I've been wanting to tell you and Mom for a while."

I took a deep breath and said, "I'm gay and in a relationship with a man. His name is Stephan Love. We're living together in town and work with a dance company called The Next Generation Dance Theatre…" I'm not sure what else I said. What I do remember is seeing Dad's face grow completely pale, and his body pull back reflexively like he was avoiding a punch.

For a few moments, all he did was sit there blinking. Then he said, "You know your mother and I can't support this…" He talked about the church's teachings; he offered to pay for therapy (I didn't bother telling him I was already in good hands), and then he told me that Stephan would never be welcome in their home. It was exactly what I expected.

Faith Trumps Family.

Our meal faded into uncomfortable silence as we waited for the check. Still, the worst was over – or so I thought. Dad went home and told my mother. The next day, he was in the hospital. One of the grafted veins from his bypass surgery a year earlier had collapsed. When my mother called to tell me, she started by saying how hurt and angry she was at not being told with Dad. She said she was worried about "how much your father could take."

Then it was my turn to get angry. I fired back, "I am not responsible for Dad's inability to handle his emotions!" And I heard my mother like I'd never heard her before. Her voice grew strong and loud as she said, "But I will do EVERYTHING I can to protect your father and take care of him!" Then she burst into tears. The conversation ended with both of us hurt, angry, and crying… and still saying "I love you," before we hung up.

I wrote a "coming out" letter and sent copies to my ten siblings, wanting everyone to hear and read the same thing from me (this was back before the days of email). Here's part of the letter:

"…I've decided I need to change, to try and reconnect with you all. In order to do this, I know I need to be honest with myself and with you, and share something personal: I am gay and have been in a relationship with a man, Stephan, for quite a while. I don't know how (or if) this will affect my relationship and interactions with each of you.

I know that I will probably feel a little uncomfortable at first, but I also know that it is important for me to be honest and real with you. I hope that if you have any questions, you'd feel okay speaking to me. I'd like to be able to talk with you openly about this.

I have this hope that eventually you'd all be able to meet Stephan. He's a wonderful, talented, intelligent man and a great friend…"

The response from my siblings was what I expected. Support from a few, a lot of nothing from the rest.

A few weeks later, Stephan and I drove out to New Hope, Pennsylvania, to hear a friend who was singing at a well-known club, opening for Livingston Taylor. It was after midnight when we finally began the drive back into town. Having grown up in the area, I told Stephan I should drive, that I knew a few shortcuts. He didn't argue. In fact, he just turned up the radio and put his head back and said, "It's all yours." Windows down, one of our mix tapes playing, we drove past sleeping farms while Joni and Phoebe sang.

Half an hour later, I was nudging Stephan's leg and saying, "I have a surprise for you." I had parked on a quiet street in a dark, sleeping neighborhood, shut the motor off, and pointed across the street. "That's the house I grew up in."

He was speechless. He just got out of the car and kept staring at my family's house, not saying a word, and not missing a single detail. Like thieves in the night, we snuck down the driveway into the backyard. I pointed out different things, whispered quick little stories from my childhood as we walked around – the creek that rolled into the woods behind our house where we used to hunt for crayfish, the garden I used to take care of – looking sad and grave-like in the darkness, the big lumpy roots of the maple we used as home base for kick ball.

I told him the story of the winter when it snowed more than two feet and we made snow forts as big as igloos and staged massive snowball fights. For a while, we stood under the big maple and just listened to the different sounds, holding hands – it was a wonderful, terribly sad moment. As we walked back to the car, we peeked in the kitchen window like two kids at a bakery counter, eyes just able to look past the windowsill into this world that I used to belong to and that Stephan would never know.

It was the closest I could bring him, and the furthest away I'd ever felt.

AIDS Timeline #9

"Made in God's image and likeness, every human person is of inestimable worth. All human life is sacred, and its dignity must be respected and protected." From *The Many Faces of AIDS*, a gospel response.

From the 1989 document, *Called to Compassion and Responsibility: A Response to the HIV/AIDS Crisis,* the bishops of the United States state, "We must keep them {those with AIDS} present to our consciousness, as individuals and a community, and embrace them with unconditional love. The Gospel demands reverence for life in all circumstances. Compassion—love—toward persons infected with HIV is the only authentic gospel response."

"A comprehensive AIDS education then has to: place AIDS within a moral context; impart accurate medical information and challenge misinformation; motivate individuals to accept the responsibility for personal choices and actions; confront discrimination and foster the kind of compassion which Jesus showed to others; model justice and compassion through policies and procedures." New Mexico Bishops, 1990

"The necessary prevention against the AIDS threat is not to be found in fear, but rather in the conscious choice of a healthy, free and responsible lifestyle." Pope John Paul II to a Vatican AIDS conference, 1989

November 23

The transfusion didn't make much of a difference. Stephan is still weak and spends his days sleeping. When he is awake, more often than not, he's staring off and I have to remind him to chew when he is eating (otherwise, he'll stare for ten minutes with the same piece of food in his mouth).

I continue to encourage him to relax, to rest. He seems to be listening. Of course, it is possible that what Stephan is going through is a direct response to the medicine he's taking. Who knows?

The other night, I got ready for work and kissed him goodnight. He looked at me and asked, "Do you mean I can let go now?" "That's right baby," I answered. The realness of that question threw me. I realized that if I was asking Stephan to let go, I had to be ready to do the same.

All of the sudden my words became my sentence. Instantly, I grew frightened and cried painful tears. If letting go is a receptive response (one of Stephan's favorite sayings), I couldn't fight what was happening. If I trusted the way of life, then it stood to reason I would not be alone with Stephan's passing, and, that I have chosen this life experience to learn and grow. Everything is okay the way it is happening; it is unfolding as it is supposed to.

At times these words provide me with comfort and a sense of peace. Other times, I can't find them; I am wrapped completely in the pain of what life and death means.

I don't know how accurate this statement is, but I have decided that when Stephan stares – or "zones out" as he calls it – he is taking a test run. He is leaving his body for brief moments, getting used to how it will feel. I can see that he is getting closer. I wish I knew the precise moment when he would pass, just so I could be ready.

November 24

I walked into the bedroom last evening to check on Stephan. When I turned on the light, he looked at me with confused eyes and whispered hoarsely, "I wet the bed. I was dreaming and couldn't wake up. I kept looking for the urinal but the lid got in the way..."

"Okay baby," I said. "Let's just get the sheets changed and everything will be all right." I helped him into a chair so I could strip the bed of the wet sheets. Sure enough, there was a large puddle staining the middle of the bed. I tried to work quickly because I knew he would get cold. I threw a bathrobe around him and he watched me work with the clean fitted sheet.

Once the bed was ready, I took a deep breath and said, "Stephan, I need you to be honest with me. Do you think you need a diaper?" This moment was bound to happen sooner or later, and I decided the best way to handle it was to just be direct and matter of fact.

"I don't know," he said. "I've thought about it for a while. I don't know." He stared at nowhere on the floor with his eyebrows raised. "I guess so," finally fell out of his mouth in a quiet whisper.

I went to the dresser for one of the diapers hidden under the T-shirts. (His sister and I decided to keep them around for exactly this moment.) I could feel my eyes burning with tears and bit my lip to keep it from quivering. I took out one of the packages and lay it on the bed. "I guess it's best if you lay down for this." I couldn't stop my tears.

They fell down my cheeks as I helped Stephan back to the bed. He lay there staring at me, his face looked vacant, his legs thin and fragile as a newborn deer. I couldn't figure out how to put the diaper on and found myself sobbing uncontrollably. "Okay," I said. My hands shook and I couldn't see through my tears. "Here we go." I stuttered as I fumbled with the fasteners and somehow managed to get everything in place.

Not until the covers were back on him did I allow myself to look at Stephan. He blinked a single tear from his right eye and all I could do was apologize. "I'm so sorry," I said, as another wave of sobs shook me.

He didn't say anything, just looked at me, then closed his eyes. I was completely drained when I finished. Nothing I ever imagined prepared me for what we went through. I knew it would get worse. I couldn't figure out what kept Stephan holding on. I didn't understand what was happening. I kept wondering, what does it take for him to say he's had enough? What am I supposed to do to help him die?

I had no answers.

November 30

I dreamt last night that Stephan was on his way somewhere. I was standing with a crowd of people, and he was about to walk out the door when he came over and said, "I almost forgot to say goodbye." His hug was strong and full of thanks. Then he turned around and walked away.

This morning, I was getting breakfast ready when Stephan called me from the bedroom. When I returned, he was hanging off the bed with his head in the trashcan, throwing up. It looked like bile and blood. He was sweating and breathing heavy. When he finished, I got him back in the bed and he said, "I was hoping I'd die in my sleep last night. I don't want to do this anymore." He fell asleep quickly after that.

His breathing was raspy and quick. I've been wondering what it will be like, that final moment when Stephan dies. Will I know? Will his soul rise slowly away from his body like so many movies suggest? Or will it just grow completely still? What will I say? What will I do? When will it happen?

I think the time is close. I'm nervous and have prayed and meditated for the patience and strength to see this through. I've got this continual headache and I'm having a hard time focusing on anything for long periods of time. I want to cry, I want to sleep. I want to get stoned, drunk and scream.

I was supposed to go visit with Mom and Dad for dinner, but I couldn't get anyone to stay with Stephan. When I called to tell Mom, she asked how I was doing. A dismissive "Okay" was the best I could offer. "Only okay?" she asked. I didn't have it in me to say anything more but was tempted to remind her that I was busy with my partner who was dying. I swallowed the first hints of anger and just said something about it being a long day.

When I think about my parents and the choices they've made, I wonder what they are learning. Then I remember I have my own lessons to learn, too, and my parents are providing me with some of the most important ones. I can't change them. I won't. I must remember over and over again to respect who they are and honor what they've given me – and hope they do the same for me.

December 2

Two or three times each night, I wake up to see if Stephan is still breathing. Sometimes I have to look real hard and listen because it's hard to tell in the dark. He decided not to continue with IV Pentam treatments. He said it was the hardest decision he ever made. He felt a lot of pressure about this, especially from me. We talked about it this morning. He didn't want to disappoint anyone, didn't want to look like he was giving up. I did my best to just listen. This really is his decision.

December 4

Yesterday morning, it took me over an hour to get Stephan and myself ready to go to the doctor's. He can't stand in the shower anymore, so I use a washcloth and basin by the bed. By the time I finished washing him, brushing his teeth, getting him dressed, and combing his hair, he was exhausted and couldn't hold himself up. He fell back on the pillows and I quickly showered and readied myself. Dr. Swartz had little to offer in terms of advice.

Stephan most likely does not have pneumonia. The shortness of breath is connected to the fact that Stephan is now anemic. All the other symptoms seem to be just the sum of the virus taking its toll on Stephan's body. Since Stephan is deciding against any further treatments, Dr. Swartz could do very little. Stephan did ask the doctor how long he thought he had to live. There were a few, long, strained moments, and finally, the doctor said a month or two.

December 8

Stephan asked for baked beans and hot dogs for our anniversary dinner (one of his favorites). He barely ate anything. I lit candles and brought in a small strawberry cream pie with two wine glasses of sparkling cider. We toasted to the past four years, both of us blinking back tears. He asked me to help him sit up and then he lay tiredly against my chest. "I just wanted to hug you," he said. We sat this way for a long time.

Stephan told me about his Mom's visit over the weekend. She told him that she tried to be a good mother and she wanted him to leave the world the way she had brought him in, peacefully. Then she had to leave the room. "She never wants us to see her cry." His tears fell silently onto the pillow; he bit his lip and talked about how he knew his mother would be okay with time.

I said that I know he loves his mother, and he replied, "But no one can know how much. People see how much I love you, too, but that's such a small part of it. It goes so much deeper."

I understood. Words can't capture what I feel for Stephan. It's larger than anything I know and sometimes weighs so heavy. Other times it lifts me so high, nothing can touch me. Complete love is powerful, so humbling. I think it's the closest thing to whatever God may be.

December 9

Thk-Pssssshhhhh. I got home from work last night and found Stephan in bed with an oxygen machine pumping next to the bed. Thk-Pssssshhhhh. The plastic tubing wound around his ears, and there were two short tubes going into each nostril. Apparently, he complained about having trouble breathing, and his mother called the doctor. A few hours later, the home health people sent out the machine. Thk-Pssssshhhhh.

I heard it pumping from the living room as I read. I heard it pumping as I brushed my teeth. I heard it pumping all night. As I waited for sleep to rescue me, I prayed that if there were a God, he would have mercy on Stephan and give him peace. Then I thought that maybe he needed strength to go through with this, so I prayed for that too.

Stephan said the tubes were uncomfortable and he didn't like them. He ended up taking them out at some point during the night. At 4:27 this morning, Stephan woke me because he had to go to the bathroom. Although he wears the diapers regularly, they are more of a precautionary measure at this point, though that may be changing quickly. I helped him position the urinal and pulled down the waistband of the diaper but his aim was less than accurate. He ended up pissing all over himself and the bed. Fortunately, he had a towel under him in case he started to sweat. I changed the towel and cleaned him off and tried to go back to sleep. I couldn't. The oxygen machine kept me awake. Thk-Pssssshhhhh.

When I finally decided to get up, it was 7:00. Stephan was soaked with perspiration, and he was cold. I turned the heat up, had a cup of coffee, and waited for the apartment to warm up so I could take care of changing the bed and him at the same time. He is resting now in clean sheets, and I am too wired to even think about getting any rest for myself.

This morning, Stephan said he didn't want the oxygen. "It's not going to help any," he whispered. His voice has become soft and kind of wheezy. "I think they were only trying to help when they got this brought in. I hope I don't disappoint them by not using it."

The holidays are almost here with their hectic expectations and forced smiles. I don't feel very merry. I'm tied up in knots. It's getting harder to take care of Stephan. He's weaker and requires more patience. He talks about things that make no sense to anyone (except him), his voice is barely audible, and he looks so used up.

Lately, I've been wondering if I'm giving him the best care. I know I could be doing more for him. I don't wash him every day; I ignore what he says. I am growing more and more resentful about what he is "doing to my life." So many times I have been ready to let him go. So many times I have said goodbye to him. So many times I have cried over this whole mess and still, he looks up at me with his brown eyes, or wakes me in the middle of the night for water.

I don't know how I'm doing it. I don't know how much longer I can.

I guess my words were too much; I started crying in the middle of the last sentence and had to stop writing.

Whenever people express their admiration or respect for "what I am doing," I try to accept what they say. There are times like now, though, when I don't feel good about any of this. It gets hard to find the love and strength that has sustained me for the past year. All I feel is sadness and a selfish wish to run away from what I have chosen.

I am not proud of wishing and praying for Stephan's death. I am not proud of the fantasies I have of my new life, knowing Stephan will not be a part of it—glad that he won't be. Sometimes I think about ways to "speed things up," or even killing him myself. As much as this "experience" can show you the good parts of who you are, it is also reveals the ugliest, darkest parts of your being. It is frightening. It is too real. It is always present.

December 18

A hospital bed was delivered and assembled yesterday. It makes it much easier when Stephan has to be fed or washed. Sleeping is strange now: I have our bed completely to myself. I can feel Stephan in the room, but he is so far away. Is it wrong that I don't mind? There's some relief in the space between us.

The past few days have been more difficult than usual, and I have felt on edge all the time. It makes me worry. I'm no good to Stephan or myself if I am resentful or angry. I know that these are "normal" feelings, but I also know that I often allow my mind to work me into an extreme state.

In my anger, I begin thinking more about my family. There is this knee-jerk reaction I feel when I think about my parents' unmoving stance towards my relationship with Stephan (and my lifestyle). There is a confusing paradox in this conflict for me. I am more and more aware of the qualities Mom and Dad have instilled in me. I am honest, committed, and feel integrity in my life that I can only say is a result of what they have taught me.

Still, in being the man they have taught me to be, I have been censored, rejected, and judged. How is their behavior Christian?!

I try to see things as they do, to accept the morality of their decisions, and respect what they have chosen, but all I can see is the hypocrisy in what they do and get angrier, judging them and making them wrong for being so dedicated to their faith. And in doing this, I am behaving like them. None of it makes any sense, and nothing gets resolved. It's a confusing, frustrating cycle.

The bottom line is I must learn to be me completely, fully, without apology. That is all I am responsible for. Mom and Dad have their own lessons to learn. I know they are just as confused about what is happening. Their faith is strong, and I'm sure they struggle with it, as well. I love them, and I know they love me.

But what happens when love is not enough?

December 19

I look in Stephan's eyes now, and I see nothing. His breathing is raspy and labored, his cheeks sunken. I don't know if he sees me – really. Still, I look into him and try to project all the love and respect I feel. For a moment, I wonder if he can feel it, then I decide it doesn't matter; it is there, it is real.

Today he said he was getting ready. He will be saying goodbye soon. My head pounds, and that too familiar knot in my throat propels me around our apartment. I check on him, give him juice, and put another load of T-shirts in the washer. I try to take deep breaths and "let go" of the anxiety I feel. Everything is happening because of what we have chosen to learn. Everything is happening just the way we planned it. Everything is okay.

Only it's not. As normal as death is, it's not okay. I try to hush the silent cry, "Why me?"

I met a gay man at work last night who said, "For every month this year, I can give you the name of someone I knew who died. My grandfather is seventy years old. He just started burying his friends. We're not supposed to be doing this at thirty. It's not what we're prepared for."

I have not been able to get those words out of my head. The truth of what this man said registers so clearly for me. I am somehow bound to their meaning. AIDS has brought a lot of people to a place we had never expected to be. Parents have buried their sons; lovers have buried lovers; friends and family have stood on the side and watched in complete confusion.

SLAVES TO THE RHYTHM

After our nighttime visit to my family's house, I felt lighter, more clear. Contact with my family dwindled to an occasional phone call to my parents, during which we stayed on safe topics, like my job and their grandchildren, and the random appearance at family get togethers and holiday meals, where I felt like an observer, disconnected and obliged at the same time. No one asked about Stephan, and I convinced myself it didn't bother me.

Meanwhile, back in town, I was grateful to be distracted by my life with Stephan, where things were in constant motion. We wrote and produced two shows a year for the dance company. We also coordinated the company's dance training by running a dance school on weekends.

I would work at my counseling job Monday to Friday, and come the weekend, I worked with Stephan and the company. Classes were Saturday mornings, followed by lunch and a little rest for the company. After that, it was either rehearsals or performances somewhere in the tri-state area.

There were some weekends when we had four performances, ran classes, and held rehearsal if we were getting close to a show – all in two days. It was nonstop work, and it was slowly paying off. The dance company and Stephan were making names for themselves.

No question, the dance company was our constant focus. But we also managed to do other fun things: We spent 10 days in Cancun, Mexico, where we climbed the Mayan pyramids in Chichen Itza and snorkeled off the reefs of Cozumel.

One summer night, we drank margaritas while watching Martha and the Vandelles perform at Penns Landing. One of my favorite nights was seeing Patti LaBelle at the Shubert. There we were, holding hands and crying as Miss Patti sang You Are My Friend. Another time, at a backyard party by the Art Museum, Stephan and I listened as Dee Dee Sharp sang" I Only Have Eyes For You" with her three back-up singers swinging behind her – amazing, just amazing.

It was a crazy, busy, funny, unending two-and-a-half years of activity before AIDS showed up. The fact that I can't remember the specifics of when and how Stephan was diagnosed says a lot about how we approached it.

I think his doctor just suggested a blood test when Stephan was in for a regular appointment. It was the late '80s, and there were more and more stories in the news about AIDS. Stephan knew his history, knew he was at risk, and thought it was a good idea.

What I do remember is not being too surprised when Stephan told me. He wasn't, either. We both decided we wouldn't let his diagnosis change how we were living. More than once, I heard Stephan say, "None of it really means anything. It's all a bunch of words." But in reality, it meant all kinds of things, starting with the condoms we now kept on the nightstand, and the uncertain future we were suddenly looking at.

A few weeks later, when I developed a sore throat, Stephan and I were trying to keep the lid on our panic. What if I had it, too? The doctor did a throat culture and said it looked like I had thrush. He looked at me very seriously and said, "You know what this means, don't you?" (Because of a compromised immune system, people with HIV/AIDS often developed thrush, a yeast infection of the mucous membrane lining the mouth and tongue). I left the office refusing to believe that I was infected, too.

It couldn't happen to both of us, could it? I kept imagining breaking the news to my family, and I was petrified. For a while, I considered leaving the country and disappearing, rather than have that conversation with my parents.

I was lucky. My blood test came back negative. We both hugged each other and cried, Stephan saying, "I don't know what I would have done… I just couldn't handle it."

We didn't waste too much time on it, though. We were too busy. We had a business to run, my counseling job, performances to rehearse for... we didn't have time to get worried. We boarded the denial train, and kept pushing forward. We were not going to let AIDS get in our way.

Besides, Stephan looked good, he felt good. We'd deal with the future when it got here. I decided not to tell my family about Stephan's diagnosis – not until it was absolutely necessary. It really wasn't hard to do, since I barely spoke with anyone. The way I saw it, the less they knew, the better. Still, it was a struggle. I was facing the most difficult thing I have ever known, and I couldn't tell my family and knew to expect little from them when I finally did.

With our game plan in place, Stephan and I kept a steady course. He ran rehearsals and scheduled performances and classes. Somehow, I ended up taking over the business side of things for the dance company and one of my first projects was to complete the application for non-profit status. It was a huge help in keeping us afloat. We had a volunteer who took over grant writing for us, and eventually, we started getting funding. It was another turning point in our dance company's development. Funders were beginning to take notice!

We decided it was time to stop renting space and open our own dance studio. We found a place on 2nd and Arch Streets in the Old City section of Philadelphia. It was an empty art gallery with a basement storage area below the studio that ran the length of the building. As we signed the lease, in the back of my mind a cloud of doubt hovered over the idea of our completing the three-year lease – what if Stephan got sick.

But I shook it off. It made good business sense to take this space, especially since we could convert the basement into an apartment and save on rent. Less than two weeks later, we had installed mirrors and a suspended floor, and Stephan and I began packing up to move into our new apartment.

The idea of our "apartment" was better than the reality of what we actually had. Our new home was little more than a cave. There were three dark, gloomy rooms in the basement resting along the right side of a long hallway that opened into the kitchen area, where a sad, muted skylight provided the only source of light for the whole downstairs. It was damp, dark, and really depressing. We tried to brighten it up with artwork and lighting, but it didn't help. But, given our financial situation, we didn't have much choice. IMPORTANT SIDE NOTE: Don't hang around the apartment during tap class. It's like sitting under a well-syncopated stampede.

Around the time we opened our studio, The Next Generation Dance Theater won a local talent competition, earning them a spot in the infamous "Amateur Night at the Apollo." Stephan was beside himself. He knew how rough the audiences could be, and he made sure the kids knew, as well. He also made sure they understood what this opportunity meant; the history of the Apollo, the other artists who performed there. This was no ordinary gig; our kids were stepping into a little bit of history.

Two weeks later, there we were, Stephan and me, holding onto each other backstage as the company tapped their way through Janet Jackson's Rhythm Nation. It was the longest three minutes that flew right by. At the end of the number, the audience was on its feet screaming and waving their hands, shouting "All right children! All right!"

We won the competition and earned a slot in the semi-finals, scheduled for the following month. It was, without question, one of the biggest moments in The Next Generation Dance Theatre's history. Things couldn't get any better!

A few weeks later, we hit the wall.

It was less than a year after being diagnosed, and Stephan was starting to look pale. He grew tired easily and was waking up at night, drenched in sweat. He went to the doctor and was diagnosed with AIDS-related pneumonia. The disease we had been hiding from finally took a seat front and center in our lives, shaking everything up. The treatment and recovery weren't pleasant, but we got through it without anyone knowing.

Stephan wanted to keep it that way. He was probably in the hospital for about a week, and then, because that cave of an apartment was not the best place for recovery, we accepted the invitation to stay with our friend Sandra for a while.

When he came out of the hospital, Stephan said that he had one goal in mind: writing and producing Slaves to the Rhythm. He didn't want to spend time dwelling on AIDS or pneumonia or his health. He was all about doing this show, period. He told me he didn't know how much time he had, and he didn't want to wake up one day wishing he had done Slaves.

So there we were, the weekend after his discharge, holed up in Sandra's guest room doing nothing but eat, sleep, and write the whole show. For the next six months, Slaves was our only focus. AIDS was still in our shadow, and it would have to stay there for a while: We were about to stage our biggest production yet. In Stephan's words, we were putting something together that Philly's dance community had never seen before.

The staging would include a pyramid shaped altar with a huge TV mounted on top. There would be a voiceover and a soundtrack and constant movement onstage at all times. The dancers played a tribe worshiping at the altar, completely reliant on the television and commanded by the voiceover. Slaves reflected the growing fascination with our talk show, tabloid-obsessed culture and the consequences of surrendering individuality to conformity.

Producing Slaves was as simple as putting your finger on mercury. Point to the goal, and watch as a thousand details roll away from you. It was endless, tiring work with dancers, choreographers, lighting and music technicians, fund-raising, costumes and rehearsals. More than once, I thought we bit off more than we could chew. But we kept pushing on. It's an incredible feeling, seeing an idea like this become reality. To see everyone coming together to support the show, and then make it even better than we imagined – Stephan and I knew we were in the middle of something special, and the kids felt it too.

Unfortunately, that kind of work doesn't come without its costs. As we got closer and closer to opening night, I started noticing some familiar, unwelcome signs. Stephan was losing weight, he was always tired, and I could hear him growing short of breath just walking down the block. By the time we entered the week of the show, the night sweats started again. At this point, we were just hoping to get through to opening night without Stephan collapsing in front of everyone. I watched him constantly, kept food nearby, and made him leave rehearsals to get rest.

On the way home from our final dress rehearsal, we sat in the back of the cab, Stephan's head feeling warm as he rested on my shoulders. He said, "I'm pretty sure I can get through this weekend and all the shows. But next week, I'm calling the doctor. He'll probably want to admit me. We can tell everyone I went to my sisters for a few days to get rest. I still don't want anyone to know."

A week later, I was on the 19th floor of Graduate Hospital reading Stephan our first review and watching him smile tiredly, his head looking small and lost in the pillows:

Philadelphia City Paper – November 16, 1992

"If performance can be judged for social and human significance, then Stephan Love's dance-theatre piece Slaves to the Rhythm deserves a rave for its clever yet straightforward attack on society's dubious priorities and the influences that foster them. Sure, it is nothing new to criticize TV, drugs, publicity and sex, especially as corrupters of youth...but in the hands of Love and his collaborators (including cowriter Terry Connell) it came across fresh and sincere...The dance, both in itself and in the dancers' execution of it was precise, intense, energetic, with jazz-dance technique alternately rapid-fire and sleazily smooth. One section was actually eerie: "Pleasure Dome," a bitter assault on drugs.

What was most remarkable about Slaves to the Rhythm was the pre-teen and teen age of most of its interpreters, which combined the forces of The Next Generation Dance Theatre and The Next Step Students (Love's groups) and YAZZU Dance Company (under Yasmin Goodman). They should have no difficulty having careers in music video, musical theatre or in some cases, a modern dance troupe (Garth Fagan, keep an eye out for these kids.)."

Susan Gould

It was the beginning of the end. Slaves ran in early November of 1992. Pneumonia would put Stephan in and out of the hospital two more times in the next two months. Christmas that year was one of the saddest, loneliest days I'd ever known. Stephan was still in the hospital; I wasn't up for pretending. I definitely wasn't feeling in the Christmas spirit. I smoked some pot, drank a little whiskey, and went to bed early. There was too much to think about. I knew what we had to do. I was just waiting for

Stephan to reach the same conclusion.

In early January, just after New Years, we called the dance company together for a meeting at the studio. I walked in with Stephan leaning on my arm and asked everyone to take a seat and shut off the music. The kids were doing the usual – practicing dance steps, goofing around, hanging out. They stopped and stared at us as we made our way into the studio.

Stephan took a seat, and in a voice barely louder than a whisper, he told the kids about his diagnosis and our decision to fold the dance company and close the studio. It had to be one of the worst moments of my life. For the past seven years, these kids grew up with each other and with Stephan. They adored him, served as his muse, and challenged him to be a better teacher.

And he became much more than their teacher. Stephan inspired their passion and showed them how to move not just on stage, but also through life. I can still hear one of the kids crying hysterically into the phone, "Stephan has AIDS Mommy! Stephan has AIDS!" Kids shouldn't know that kind of pain.

When we got home that night, it was Stephan's turn. He cried that body heaving, tears pouring down his face, can't catch your breath cry. I just held him tight and waited for him to finish. When he finally looked at me, he said, "This is the beginning of the end. You know that, don't you?"

Because our basement apartment was so damp and depressing, we didn't argue when Sandra insisted we stay with her again. Stephan was scheduled for an additional fourteen IV treatments at home, to prevent any future pneumonia infections. The first few times, I sat with him and watched the nurse hook up the medication, wondering how effective it would be.

I was always a half-assed journal writer, but once Slaves was over and Stephan went in the hospital, I began writing in my journal every day. I felt like I was swimming in deep, dangerous waters without any sense of where land was. My journal was the only thing that kept me grounded, gave me something to hold onto, and ultimately stood witness to some of the most profound, beautiful, and painful, moments in my relationship with Stephan and my life.

Every night, after he fell asleep, I'd sit at the computer and write about anything and everything. Sometimes, I would only write a sentence and then just stare at my words for endless minutes. Other times, my fingers moved across the keyboard with surprising speed, words flowing out of me like water from a faucet. When I could write no more, I'd turn off the computer and make my way to bed, grateful for what I had with Stephan and worried about a future that looked dark and full of pain.

"AIDS obliges people to think of sex as having, possibly, the direst consequences: suicide. Or murder." <u>Susan Sontag</u>

"I have learned more about love, selflessness and human understanding in this great adventure in the world of AIDS than I ever did in the cut-throat, competitive world in which I spent my life." <u>Anthony Perkins</u>

"AIDS is not just God's punishment for homosexuals; it is God's punishment for the society that tolerates homosexuals." <u>Jerry Falwell</u>

"The slow-witted approach to the HIV epidemic was the result of a thousand years of Christian malpractice and the childlike approach of the church to sexuality. If any single man was responsible, it was Augustine of Hippo who murdered his way to sainthood spouting on about the sins located in his genitals." <u>Derek Jarman</u>

"We're all going to go crazy, living this epidemic every minute, while the rest of the world goes on out there, all around us, as if nothing is happening, going on with their own lives and not knowing what it's like, what we're going through. We're living through war, but where they're living it's peacetime, and we're all in the same country." <u>Larry Kramer</u>

December 22

Nothing changes, Stephan keeps holding on. I don't understand it. I want to know why his life is ending the way it is. What is it that he still has to do or learn before he can leave? I see a marked difference in him. He is speaking incoherently all the time, he is always uncomfortable, but still he hangs on, making it through another day.

I keep reminding myself to accept what is happening. Most times I feel like I'm doing okay. Still, there is this need to know the "why's" and "when's" of my life. I also find myself battling an impatient feeling, wanting to get on with what I want to do. In a way, my life has been in a terminal holding pattern. Still, if I believe in the importance of life choices and lessons, then, like Stephan, I am not finished with this lesson.

My life within this disease goes on, mostly because of the help of friends and Stephan's family. It's amazing how we get through each day. There is a mindless cadence I have been following, one of motion without direction. Each day passes into the next, Stephan is taken care of, and sometimes I get a chance to breathe, as well.

Creatively, I feel so stunted and uninspired. I look at the stories I have been working on and find no voice to work with. Half-started, half-finished, my mind feels empty when I look at them.

I wonder if Stephan thinks about what is happening outside the bedroom. I wonder if he knows how many people are waiting, paralyzed, trying to carry on. He says he wants to go. He says he wonders why God won't take him. Then, when I try to talk to him about how everyone is okay and we'll miss him, he gets angry and says he doesn't want anyone telling him when to leave.

Friends are upset by the amount of pain and discomfort Stephan is in. I find myself working to make him as comfortable as he can be, but I don't think about how it must hurt – not anymore. It's not that I don't care, I just know there's little I can do. I guess I've become numb.

December 24

I have come to realize that my life has developed a two dimensional scope. I swing back and forth between feeling love and acceptance and frustration and anger. Being with Stephan is easy when I am in touch with love. I can sit with him and talk with him. When I am not with him, I am still able to go through the rest of my day feeling calm and sure about the direction I am moving in.

Then there are times when I can't find that love. My eyebrows are constantly pulled together, and my head pounds dully all day. I feel impatient about everything and I have no tolerance for the demands Stephan makes of me.

I wonder why it is hard to hold onto love. I guess that is part of the human experience, though I'm not sure I understand the necessity of it. Here I am in my life, struggling to keep my thoughts and feelings positive, as I watch someone slowly die. Selfishly, I want him to hurry up because he is keeping me from what I see as my future plans. This lack of tolerance feeds on itself and soon I am having difficulty with others who I don't even know.

In my meditations, I pray for understanding and the strength to stay within love. Today, I found out how powerful love could be. With Stephan becoming less coherent, it is more and more difficult to understand him. Typically, I want to hush him as I leave the room, like a parent does a child. Tonight, I decided not to be so quick to leave the room, to not be so selfish. I listened and stayed with him.

I said, "I remember the first time we met. You were taking a dance class with Finn. Do you remember?" We started talking about when we first met and some of our early experiences. We ended up smiling and my heart felt lighter than it had in a long time.

I don't know how this translates into other situations. When I think about doing this with my family, I feel less sure of myself and see a less receptive audience. Love is lost before I have even begun any interaction. I still don't have the reasons why, but I now have a better understanding of the how. As I discover these thoughts and feelings, I can get why Stephan has not gone yet: It's these very lessons.

December 27

Christmas happened like it did every year. I tried to keep it simple, and for the most part it was. Stephan's family came by with food and gifts. They visited for a while in the morning and left quietly as Stephan fell asleep in bed. Different friends stopped by throughout the day and, although tiring, it was okay. For a while, Stephan even joined us, though he didn't last too long.

One of the worst side effects of Stephan's medication is constipation. He will go days without taking a dump. But when his bowels start moving, it is one of the most painful experiences for him. Lately, I've been giving him suppositories. He lies on the bed with terrible cramps waiting for the suppository to work. Then, I half carry, half drag him to the portable pot when he says he has to go. Once on the pot, he holds my hands so he doesn't fall and pushes so hard he loses his breath.

More than once, I thought he was going to have a heart attack. We used to joke that he knew what women went through during labor. Now he's too tired, too weak to find humor in it. Christmas day, after three attempts that involved lifting him from the bed to the pot and back three times and staying with him so he didn't fall, he finally took a successful shit and grunted, "Merry Christmas" as a single turd hit the bottom of the bucket.

Afterwards, he was exhausted. I carried him back to bed, cleaned him, and put a fresh diaper on him. I'm still learning how to keep my mind completely focused on what I am doing, and I stifle my tears. In my head, I hear my voice coaching me through each step.

Once Stephan is resting, the voice speaks again, "Now clean everything up. Use bleach on the bucket. Put the dirty rag in the washer. Take off your plastic gloves and wash your hands..."

I feel empty as I go through these motions. All the while, friends are out in the living room pretending it's a nice Christmas. Once Stephan was in bed, and I took a few moments to get myself together, then I went back out and joined everyone else in the living room acting like it was, indeed a Merry Christmas.

When everyone finally left, I lay down on the couch for a nap only to be called into the bedroom by Stephan. His feet and legs were hurting him so much that the weight of the blanket on his toes was sending sharp stabbing pains through him. I rubbed his feet with lotion until he fell asleep.

That evening, Stephan was unusually lucid, and for a moment, it almost felt like he was his old self. He kissed me affectionately and held my hand. He told me I was handsome and how much he loved me. He said he was beginning to understand why I loved him and thanked me for everything I had done for him.

"One day, you're going to wake up, and I'll be gone. Just like that," he said, and tears welled up in his eyes. "I wish I knew when so I could be ready. You could be, too." I rubbed his hand and asked if he wanted anything in particular done for his memorial service, and he said no. He took my hand and laughed, saying that I was so easy about everything.

"Everyone always asks me how I do it," I said, my tears falling. "I just love you. That's it. It's not hard. Loving you is not hard." My words hit me, and I sobbed uncontrollably. The light in the bedroom was soft, and Stephan seemed peaceful. I looked at him and he smiled through his own tears and said, "I know what you mean."

Two days later, my family's Pollyanna party was at my parents' house. I don't know how to describe what it was like to see my family. I drove there looking forward to seeing everyone, which was an unexpected sensation, to be positive about a family visit. When I walked in the door, I got a big, long hug from my mother, the standard handshakes from my brothers. My sisters and in-laws were their usual warm selves. I looked around the room and wondered what was going through everyone's minds. I couldn't tell what was behind the strained smiles: concern, fear, both?

My nieces and nephews, some of whom I haven't seen in over a year, took a while to warm up to this strange man with a beard and earring. As usual they provided more than enough distraction to keep everyone preoccupied. I quickly ran upstairs to wrap my gifts and was overwhelmed by how small, almost foreign, the house felt.

I found Dad downstairs watching the football game; he gave a big "Hey!" as I walked into the rec room. He hugged me and asked if I wanted anything to drink. "Just keep pretending," I said to myself. Everyone moved from the kitchen to the living room to the Rec Room and back again, talking and eating and playing with the kids.

I followed suit, making small talk and trying to enjoy myself. They all seemed happy, genuinely happy. Conversation and laughter washed over me in waves, leaving me always feeling a little off-center. Sometimes I found myself sitting and watching what was happening, then someone would sit next to me and ask, "How's work going?" Work? No one asked about Stephan, except my mother, who did it quietly, quickly, undercover. What are they afraid of?

"My partner is dying," I wanted to say. "I'm a little afraid, but I'm also learning about how powerful love is." Then my niece interrupts or someone takes a picture and I am brought back to the fact that no one speaks this language, at least not in my parents' house with everyone else around.

I love my family. I enjoy the way we can all laugh and play into each other's humor. I know they love me, too. We are beautiful despite our shortcomings. And in spite of the distance I felt, I had fun and was glad I went.

Mom and Dad walked me to the car I borrowed. None of us had a jacket on, and it was very cold. I put my arm around Mom's shoulder, and she wrapped her hand around my waist. Dad walked ahead of us and remarked on how nice the car was. "It looks new," he said. I said something about it being less than a year old.

I hugged them both, thought about saying, "I love you," but didn't. I'm not sure I know why. What I wanted to say, was, "Stephan will be dead soon." That, too, was left unsaid. As I got in the car, I could see them standing, arms around each other. I felt their love, and their concern. I didn't say anything; there really was nothing to say. I couldn't save them from their fears any more than they could save me from mine. I honked the traditional "shave and a haircut," and drove away, wiping away the tears that burned my eyes.

January 3

We had a "family meeting" on Friday. I told everyone my thoughts about placing Stephan in hospice care. I sat on the floor and spelled out everything: Stephan's rapidly deteriorating health, the work involved in taking care of him, and my exhaustion. Stephan's mother responded first saying, "I understand what you're saying. You've done right by him up 'til now. I think it's the best thing, they can take good care of him in a home." She moved like a little bird, her head bobbing up and down as she talked. I knew how she felt. In fact, she told one of Stephan's sisters that she didn't know how I had managed to do as much as I had for so long. She said Stephan would have given in long ago if the shoe were on the other foot. It was quite a relief having her blessing.

At some point, we heard Stephan shouting from the bedroom, "I know what you're doing! I know it ALL!" We gathered around the hospital bed, and he began stammering through something no one could understand. Then he called for me.

When I took his hand, he began to cry sad tears and said he knew how hard things were for me but that he didn't want to go live in a home. There was such a determination in his voice, a mournful request. "I'm running out of steam, baby," I said. "I need a little break. I know you understand." My voice cracked, and I wasn't sure I'd be able to finish without losing control. I told him we had more talking to do. Nothing had been set in place; we were just looking at options.

Everyone stood around in this dazed connection that these moments offer, wiping away silent tears. "It's going to be all right," I said, and kissed his forehead. "Everything's going to be all right."

It is now three days later. I've begun sorting through clothes and papers looking for what's no longer important. Plans have changed, for now. Stephan's sister wants him to stay with her for a while, hospice care will be decided later. I wasn't about to argue. As far as I was concerned, any change would be a good one — for us both.

I found a copy of the photo album we gave to the dance company last Christmas. There's a picture of Stephan and me at a Slaves rehearsal. In it, Stephan looks vibrant, happy, so much himself. The kids are dancing or posing for the camera, their faces part of a lost world where life seemed almost enchanted.

As Stephan slept in the bedroom, I read the quote under the picture at the end of the photo album. I don't know where it came from: "Without dreams, there is no need to work hard. Without hard work, there is no need to dream. Dream on!!"

January 7

There seems so little to write about now. Or at least I don't have the energy to sit and write anything. I try to keep myself busy during the day, reading or trying to organize the apartment for my eventual move. I took three days to look at apartments around town. I've decided on one up on 13th Street. It's small but clean, and the location is convenient to everything.

I'm supposed to move in the first of February. Stephan will go to his sister's house sometime around the 26th of this month, assuming he doesn't decide to leave before then.

Most of his days are now spent sleeping or staring out into that middle of nowhere he's found. He doesn't even recognize me when I come in the room. Feeding him is almost impossible. He'll get a mouthful of food and chew once, and then he'll start staring again. It took me over half an hour to get him to eat a few bites of a muffin.

I think most of this is brought on by the painkillers he's taking, not that I'm complaining. Stephan looks at peace when he stares – he is definitely not in any pain.

I keep hoping I have the strength and patience and find myself being tested on it more and more. This morning, Stephan woke me up at 4:30 because he thought he had to be somewhere. I got him to fall asleep again, and for the next five hours, I half slept, half listened to his mindless talking. He thought there was something under his bed; he wanted to call his friends; he was talking to someone, I'm not sure whom.

This morning, when I checked on Stephan, he was completely soaked. "I didn't do it," Stephan said with these big, innocent eyes. "Don't worry about it baby," I said, and changed his diaper and the bed sheets.

I look at his face, tired and thin, and I wonder what it feels like inside his body. Where does he go when he stares like that? What does he see? Yesterday, as I got ready for work, I sat on my bed and put on my shoes and talked to him. "I'm having a hard time today. I've been on the phone with landlords and throwing away stuff we don't need. I spoke with your mom and sisters. I feel like I'm alone in this. I miss you today." He continued looking out the window and I stifled the burning sensation in my throat and left for work.

January 9

Stephan's got bedsores, and they're getting worse and worse. I can see the purple bruise growing from under the open sore at the very base of his spine. I try to keep Stephan on his side, but he complains of not being able to breathe and rolls back so the pressure again sits on the base of his spine in that same spot again.

I feel like there is something else I should do. I apologize to Stephan all the time for not taking better care of him. Sometimes he understands me and says he knows I'm doing the best I can. I feel like I'm not. Often, I hide out in the living room, reading.

I hope he's going to die soon, holding tight to this rational voice telling me it's okay to feel like this. For a while, I can believe myself.

I tip toe into the bedroom, hoping he doesn't hear me or I hide my disappointment when his eyes are wide open, looking directly at me. I offer him water and rub his arm. Yesterday, he didn't know who I was, his eyes scared and unsure of me. He moves in and out of this dementia, grimacing when he tries to move his legs. He talks about people he sees behind me. If these people are "from the other side," I hope they take good care of him.

Stephan's pain patch has been increased, and he still takes another pain medication a few times a day to supplement this. Small bruises are forming on his heels now, too. I guess they are also bedsores. He talks more about going home and moans painfully that he can't do it any more. I changed his diaper this afternoon and winced with every groan he let out. Still, he's here. I wish I just knew why. What is left for him to learn? What is left for me to learn?

I took myself to the movies this afternoon, since there was nothing I could do, and I have to continue acting like I know what it means to "take care of myself." Truthfully, the time away helps, but it also feels like a tease. Each time I return, I still have to face that elevator and swallow this feeling that I wish I were someone else.

The apartment pulls me in, and I quietly walk back into the bedroom to see how Stephan is. In the faint light, I find him breathing softly, relieved that he is asleep. For the moment, there is nothing I can do.

January 13

Stephan needs to go back to the hospital. This was the best solution. He needed more help than I or anyone else could give him. With his mom's support, I called the doctor and made arrangements to have him admitted tomorrow morning. The weight of this moment hit me hard. "He won't be coming back," I said to the empty living room, and I lost it, again. I sank to the floor of the living room and gave myself over to more tears. Stephan and I would not be together anymore.

Our last night together, we watched TV – at least, I did; Stephan murmured to himself in between sleeping. I told him what was going to happen in a few hours, but I wondered if he understood. Finally, around one o'clock, I turned off the TV and sat by the hospital bed. Stephan was staring at nothing; his breath was shallow and quick.

I thanked him for believing in me, for his patience, and the memories we created. I talked about Cancun and the snorkeling trip we took, The Apollo Theater, and my birthday in New York. I talked a lot about the dance company and the shows we produced. Then, I apologized through sloppy tears for what was about to happen.

Through sobs, I told him how tired I was, how he was too sick for me or for any of us to take care of him anymore. I don't know if he heard my words, but I continued talking, anyway. I asked him to forgive me for anything I had done that hurt or disappointed him. When my tears finally stopped, I rested my head on his hand and took a deep breath.

Completeness surrounded us. We rested in nothing less than love – and then I cried harder at the incredible beauty of it.

January 14

I woke up early, fixed myself some coffee, and took a deep breath. I called Stephan's sister, told her I was getting ready to call the ambulance. Then I dialed 911, gave the operator the necessary information, hung up, and waited. I held Stephan's hand and didn't say a word. When, not two minutes later, sirens echoed down Third Street, I knew they were for us.

The first person to respond was a cop. He asked what the problem was, and I felt the slight stir of anger as he winced when I said, "My partner has AIDS. He's very sick. I need to get him to the hospital."

He said he needed to see Stephan and walked back to our bedroom asking why I couldn't get Stephan there on my own. I was not in the mood to argue with this man; I didn't respond. He'd understand once he saw Stephan. I lit a cigarette and waited in the living room for the ambulance to arrive.

The ambulance technicians worked quickly getting Stephan onto the stretcher. Unfortunately, it wouldn't fit into the bedroom because of the way the apartment is set up, so they carried Stephan out of the bedroom using the bed sheets like a sling. Stephan groaned loudly, "No!" and I saw him wincing and wiggling around in pain. Once on the stretcher, Stephan was wheeled out into the hallway, and I followed them to the elevator, where we ran into our next hurdle.

The elevator was too narrow to fit the stretcher with Stephan lying down, so they moved Stephan into a seated position and locked the gurney in place. All the while, he shouted "No! No! NO!" It was awful and only got worse when I realized that I couldn't fit in the elevator.

I had to hear Stephan's repeated cries and moans rising up and echoing through the stairwell as I walked down the seven flights. When I finally got to ground level, the stretcher was already at the ambulance. By that point, I think, Stephan was in shock. He probably didn't weigh more than 110 pounds now – down from175. His face looked almost skeletal. He stared straight ahead, looking extremely small and old as they lifted him.

I'm sure I rode with him in the ambulance. I have a vague memory of looking out the back window, sirens screaming around me, but really I don't remember it. What I do remember is meeting with his doctor, who was brief and certain. "We're not looking at much more time here. I'm putting him on a morphine drip so that he's not in pain. Other than that, there's not much more to do." I just nodded my head. There wasn't much more to do.

I spent the rest of the morning trying to feel something but couldn't. I walked around the apartment thinking about how sad it was, but I only felt numb. Finally, a picture of Stephan flashed through my mind. He was sitting on the stretcher, waiting for the ambulance drivers to open the doors. He looked so lost, so beaten.

I couldn't get this picture out of my mind and I kept saying, "It's okay baby, it's okay." For what felt like hours, I lay on the floor moaning and holding my stomach. I couldn't stop. Rocking back and forth, I realized I didn't have to stifle my sobs for fear of Stephan's hearing. For the first time, I mourned freely, openly, loudly, until I finally lay there too exhausted to move.

The silence in the apartment felt unbelievably large and I lay there listening. There were no soft moans from the bedroom, no raspy breaths, no rustling of sheets looking for the most comfortable position for his legs. Silence so big it was unsettling.

I slept okay last night. I spent the rest of the day looking out the window smoking or trying to get organized. Tears escape me for the moment and I have the radio on to fight the cavernous silence. Friends have been calling to see how I am and to remind me to take care of myself. I called the people to come get the hospital bed. I emptied another closet.

I thought about joining a gym on my way to the hospital and I still have to write a letter to my landlord explaining the circumstances around our breaking the lease. I can't explain how different everything is now, how out of control I feel, how much I don't care.

January 16

"Death seems imminent, one to two days." This was the way the doctor ended his note yesterday. Not that I should have been reading Stephan's chart, but I did every other time he was in the hospital, so I helped myself again. Stephan hated this little habit of mine, but I felt better having a more concrete explanation. Stephan's doctor has been more than helpful. It was especially nice to see the respect he gave Stephan and me as a couple. I wonder how it must feel, working with a terminal patient, especially one like Stephan.

Does he cry sometimes at night? What does he think about our relationship? How does he feel seeing someone die, knowing that medically there is nothing left he can do?

Yesterday, when I walked into Stephan's room, who do I see sitting by the bed but Finn. It turns out Finn is now a nurse at Graduate Hospital and works on the floors below. He saw Stephan's name on one of the computers the day he was admitted and has been coming up to see him every day. And so it comes full circle... the man who introduced me to Stephan is here to help me say goodbye.

I keep walking around our apartment, looking at everything, not sure what to do next. I'm too tired to cry, but I know it's there. Some old friends of Stephan's were in town, and I met them for a drink. Their company was a welcome distraction, though what we talked about, I have no clue. Somehow, they would get me into the conversation, and somehow, I would find myself responding to questions, though my voice sounded monotone in my ears, my eyes were mostly staring over their shoulders waiting for the night to be over, when I could go home and sleep.

Stephan's mom came and took the clothes I decided to get rid of. I also gave her the plants, since she took better care of them than we ever did. Other stuff has gone to his sisters and niece. It feels like I am scraping away, layer by layer, everything I can about what will soon be my "old life."

Emptiness surrounds me, fills me, and consumes me. There is nothing left but tears. I am amazed at how quickly and often I cry. Tears welcome me on the couch in the living room and sing to me over the radio. They wait for me in the coldness of my bed and laugh with me at pictures of days gone by. I can't fight them, I don't even try anymore. I just give in. Eventually, they're over, and I find something to distract me until the next crying jag.

January 18

Stephan died this morning at 1:35. His sister called to tell me.

"Have you heard?" she asked. "Stephan died about fifteen minutes ago."

I couldn't figure out what to do. I sat in bed, looking out the window, feeling like I should do something but not sure what. I didn't cry, at least not right away. I thought about a cigarette and a drink but didn't feel like going out. I thought about how Stephan looked when I last saw him. There is no question he is much better off now, but I couldn't feel that, either. I couldn't find my tears, I couldn't feel relief. All I felt was a confused numbness.

Finally, after a few cigarettes and a drink, I began calling friends. They asked if I wanted company. I didn't. I got up, made tea, and sat on the couch. As I stared out the window, eventually I found my tears, or they found me.

It's now 3:30 in the morning, and I am exhausted, relieved, and totally clueless about what happens next.

January 22

I have lived three life times in the past few days. I have been reluctant to write, mostly because it is hard to find words to describe what has happened. My reluctance also stems from the realization that my next entry would be the final one for this part of my life. I don't know which is harder: endings or beginnings.

Amazingly, with the help of an incredible group of friends, I moved into my new apartment this week. They literally did everything: organized, packed, drove, carried boxes, and told me what to do. I was clueless. The move was a good distraction for me, though I still find myself crying and confused.

The Wednesday after all the big stuff was moved, I walked back to our apartment to grab a few things. On my way, I realized this would be the last time I'd be in our place, the last time I'd be in a space that Stephan and I shared. When I opened the door, my mind was filled with intense memories. I saw Stephan walking through the empty apartment when we first found it. He loved how bright it was and the view of the Ben Franklin Bridge. He also liked the privacy of the bedroom in the back of the apartment.

I saw Stephan sitting in his favorite spot on the couch, where he could see the lights running up and down the cables of the bridge. He'd wrap himself in an afghan and sit quietly for what seemed like hours. I'd lost count of how many times. When he could no longer walk out on his own, he'd lean heavily on my arm and reach for his spot on the couch with relief.

It was getting late, and the light was starting to fade, and there I stood in the middle of the living room, eyes closed and singing to myself the Roberta Flack song that Stephan said made him think of me, "You Who Brought Me Love". I cried as I moved around in a slow circle, trying hard to find Stephan, to feel him just once more. Then, I remembered the last time we made love. Despite the fact that he had lost the energy and desire for physical affection, one night he reached for me and reminded me of how sensual love could be. It was one of the most selfless experiences I'll ever know.

I hesitated walking back to the bedroom – so much happened back there in the last few months. It's hard to describe the energy I felt in there. This room became Stephan's refuge and his prison. I pulled a chair into the exact position of where Stephan lay. My heart was racing, and there were all these images going through my mind of his last weeks at home. In that moment, I realized that slowly, without question or doubt, he had surrendered his life to me. He trusted me completely. "I understand!" I called to him. "I know how much you loved me! I know. Thank You! Thank You!" And again, my tears fell in waves.

I often said to Stephan that if there were a way, I expected a visit with him after he died. I know Stephan was with me in the room. I could feel him. I could even smell him. He was with me, and I couldn't stop crying. I didn't want to. My tears were filled with thanks and love, fear and sadness, and the incredible beauty that was us.

I have no idea how long I stayed in the bedroom. Eventually, I said goodbye to Stephan. I sent him on his way and walked out of the apartment feeling weightless and exhausted.

January 23

Today we had Stephan's memorial service. Aside from a few small suggestions from me, his sister handled the whole service and organized a celebration that truly represented who Stephan was. To try and summarize what was said would not be fair to the experience of the memorial service. The church was filled with so many different people.

I was especially pleased – and surprised – that some of my family attended. There couldn't have been a better opportunity for them to know who Stephan was and who we were together.

I listened to everyone speaking and singing of the life and love that was Stephan, and I fell in love with him all over again. Stephan would have been embarrassed by all the praise and emotions shared, but in his absence, everyone shined, and so did he. I spoke last and ended with the following excerpt from Stephan's journal:

MY IDEAL

March 11, 1989

To fully know, understand and consciously live my birthright as an aspect of the one mind (God); To live free from fear; To express love through patience, kindness, understanding, and joy, For perfect balance and harmony in spirit, mind, and body; to truly know and experience the meaning of Joy, Beauty and Peace of Mind; To touch every soul with the message of love; To experience abundance; To be a clear channel for creative energy to flow through; To know and completely experience the joy, beauty and satisfaction in my accomplishments be them big or small; To hear clearly my intuitive voice and to follow without question.

Then, I asked the dance company to come to the front of the church, and I put on the song, "The Only Way is Up," and as if on cue, the kids broke into a dance routine they learned from Stephan. Eventually, everyone was in the aisle dancing. I think it was the kind of ending Stephan would have liked.

MY YEAR OF FIRSTS

My year of firsts began the moment I closed the door to my apartment and sat by myself after Stephan's memorial service.

This was my first time truly being alone, feeling alone. My apartment, this dark, depressing one-bedroom on Spruce Street with a window opening flatly onto the black-red bricks of the building next door, was another first: my first place without him. I stared at the ceiling on my first night without Stephan and considered all the other firsts that lay ahead of me in the coming months. I imagined waking up tomorrow, the first morning, and gratefully checking that one off the list.

Next, I moved the clock forward to see what my first weekend would look like… first week, month. Everything ahead of me felt empty, far away, and layered in loneliness.

My first night without Stephan was torturous. When I finally went to bed, my mind wouldn't stop rolling from one thought to another. Fortunately, I preempted sleep problems by smoking some weed and drinking a little whiskey and ginger before going to bed. I also found a soundscape CD with humpback whales; it was one of many presents Stephan got from friends hoping to help in some small way. I played it on repeat all through the night, falling asleep listening to those sweet, sad sounds. For the next year, that CD would be my security blanket. I couldn't fall asleep without it.

I decided to take a month and regroup before I went back to work. My first week, I mostly cried, smoked cigarettes and weed, and slept. It was all I wanted to do. It was all I had energy for. I could pull it together for a little while and meet with friends for dinner or to talk on the phone, but when I was by myself in my apartment, I would collapse in waves of tears over and over and over, then make my way to bed.

There was an odd intoxication to those moments, the intensity of the emotion, the extreme physical sensations my body generated. It was addictive, and I wanted all of it. Actually, what I wanted most, what I craved, was the quiet after the storm. I welcomed the numbing exhaustion following each crying jag, when my mind would go blank and I could finally rest.

There were a few nights in that first month when I'd wake up screaming, and others where I'd remember a word or gesture, and a sense of calm would settle over me like a blanket, warm and comforting. I stopped trying to understand what was happening, and just let it happen.

As the days went by, I could feel these meltdowns grow less intense, less frequent. My sleep was getting deeper, less restless. I joined a gym and decided to quit smoking. I went to the movies a few times, walked around our old neighborhood a lot (probably too much), sometimes crying, sometimes just standing outside of different places, watching and listening to the ghosts of another life: our dance studio (now an art gallery), our old apartment on Fifteenth and Green, one of our favorite restaurants, even the laundry mat could inspire a quick burst of sobs when I walked past.

As the first month came to a close, I was slowly beginning to feel more centered and started looking forward to finding a job. It was time for a little more structure.

My first job in my new role as AIDS Widow would be a return to my roots. Through the help of a friend still working at The Horsham Clinic, I was offered a Social Worker position back on the Adolescent Unit. What a difference a few years, and managed care, could make in the mental health industry. When I left The Horsham Clinic, the average length of stay for a child was probably about three months. That was a significant amount of time and really provided for effective, sustainable changes in a patient's (and the family's) behavior. In less than five years, the average length of stay had dropped to fourteen days.

This new model was geared toward stabilization of the crisis, usually with medications, followed by outpatient programming, which was a much less expensive solution. I had my doubts about how effective this paradigm was.

I didn't like the bottom-line mentality being used to dictate treatment, especially given the severity of the problems these kids had.

But outpatient and partial programming was where the money for treatment was going, and the industry followed. I really didn't care one way or another. I was relieved to have a job again. Anything was better than sitting home crying and smoking all day. For now, it really wasn't important that I liked it. I just needed some kind of starting point from which to build. If I had to, I'd look for another job later.

I could feel the tears of relief rising when I was called and offered the position. All I could think was, "It's going to be okay... I'm going to be okay." As the woman from Human Resources went through a few final details about the starting date, salary, and benefits, I flopped into a chair, barely listening, eyes closed, feeling myself really relax for the first time – another first – since Stephan passed. I had been saved. My money situation was bleak, at best. It was still questionable whether I'd have enough to hold me until my first paycheck. But there was a paycheck in my future.

Then I heard her say, "The last thing we need to do is schedule your drug screen." My heart slammed into my ribs and I stopped breathing. "Really? When did this start?" I hoped I sounded as cool as I tried to be. It was part of the new hiring system put into effect after a large corporation had bought the hospital.

I quickly made up a story about heading out of town later that day, and was told in no uncertain terms that if I couldn't make it in for a drug screen within the next twenty-four hours, the job offer would be rescinded. I got off the phone and went right to the gym, and worked on the treadmill for an hour. Drinking water and jogging, trying to sweat as much as possible. Then, I sat in the sauna until I thought I would pass out and came home to crash for a few hours. I went back to the gym again in the evening for another hour of cardio. I kept drinking as much water as I could, even through the night, waking up hourly to go to the bathroom.

By some miracle, I passed my first drug screen and began my brief, second life at The Horsham Clinic. It was a frantic, tense environment on The Adolescent Unit, where the administration was constantly out on marketing calls to schools and unions and wherever else they may be able to dig up a referral source. Case presentations weren't focused on the patient's pathology and behavior across different modalities. They were businesslike and all about the facts: how much coverage was there, what were the discharge plans.

I wasn't a therapist anymore; I was a paper pusher. And I didn't care. I couldn't care. I had a job, I had benefits, and pushing papers was a hell of a lot better than waiting tables.

Once my job was in place, I was ready for my first conversation with my parents. One of the bigger firsts that I knew I had to take care of, and the only one I really dreaded. Birthdays and holidays – they would be sad, and difficult, but I wasn't afraid of them. Actually, it wasn't fear that tugged at me when I thought about seeing my folks; it was regret. Regret at an outcome I knew I couldn't avoid.

I was on a bit of a fool's errand really, like a man yelling in anger at a mountain because it won't get out of his way. I knew my parents. I knew their commitment to their faith. And I knew that no matter what I said, I'd leave their house at the end of the night confused and angry at a devotion to faith I didn't have.

I purposely waited until after I got a job to call. I didn't want to walk into their house from a place of need. Instead, I showed up feeling both defiant and vulnerable. We had dinner, just the three of us, all huddled at one end of the ten-foot table, pretending not to feel self conscious, trying to remember how to be with each other. Fortunately, with a big family, there was plenty to talk about. We ate dinner and I caught up on what was happening with my brothers and sisters.

Once the plates were cleared, the real conversation began. I took a deep breath and started by asking them how they could choose not to help one of their children who was in pain. Mom said, through tears, "I knew you were in pain. Believe me, I knew. We knew. Your father and I were in pain, too. You think it was easy to do what WE did?"

It was Dad who quickly stepped in, logical, by the book Dad who pulled us from the emotional firing line into black and white with the same litany of sin and church I'd heard for years. They could accept that I was gay. The church had no problems with homosexuality: it was only a problem when it became expressed in a relationship. He repeated: Mom and he wouldn't allow it in their house, and again, he offered to help pay for therapy if I wanted it.

I said, "Don't worry, Dad. I've got it taken care of. And for what it's worth, being gay is okay in his world." Then it was my turn to cry, "I was everything you taught me to be. You would have been so proud of me. And you missed it."

Mom looked at me with surprising anger and said, "We never taught you to act like that. Not in our house!" I couldn't believe how she chose to hear what I had said. I looked at her and said, "I was selfless, patient, forgiving, strong. These were the things you taught me. And you didn't see any of it. You missed a chance to be there with me. To HELP me. How can you hold onto a faith that won't let you see any of that?" I was barely holding it together and finished saying, "And when I think about how the future looks for me in our family, all I can see ahead of me are moments where we keep missing each other."

There was nothing left to say. Nothing left to do. I left the house that night at a loss. I loved these people. That hadn't stopped. But how could I maintain a connection with my parents with such an incredible tear in the fabric of our relationship? How did we recover from something like this?

For the most part, it was just same song, different verse. We fell back into the same pattern of communication in place from when Stephan and I were together. I phoned on occasion, and we talked about my job and the rest of the family. I visited with the family every few months, feeling a bit like I did when Stephan and I snuck into my parents' backyard just a few years earlier. I was looking in on something familiar while not really being a part of it.

I was amazed at how some of my siblings would not say a word about what I had been through or ask how I was coping. It was a weird, two-dimensional connection that we all tried to make feel okay. But it was all too close to the surface for me. I felt raw and exposed – and ignored. It was better if I stayed away.

No matter. There were more important things to focus on. I knew I wasn't going to stay in Philly. That was pretty clear within the first few weeks of being on my own. I couldn't. There were too many shadows haunting me at street corners and familiar faces filled with expectant sympathy. I wanted to find a place where I didn't have a history. And I needed to create distance between me, and my family. The fact that I didn't like my job and felt suffocated in my stale apartment only added fuel to this desire. Change was coming, but it would take another six months and a few more firsts before I had a plan.

My goal was to be out of the city before the biggest first of all – the anniversary of Stephan's death. Birthdays and holidays were as hard and emotional as I expected them to be, but nothing compared to what I had been through. I was moving on, and that realization was a relief – and a source of upset. I didn't want to forget, but I hated remembering.

I took care of my first sex after Stephan with a practical mindset. I knew it would happen. I could either sit around, imagining what it would be like, or I could just get it over with. Maybe two weeks after Stephan died, I decided to take care of it. I went to a bar called Woody's with one thing in mind: get first sex off the list. Enter Robert. He was a handsome, muscular guy I saw standing by the dance floor. I took him back to my apartment, trying to avoid any conversation by making out with him every twenty feet as we walked down Thirteenth Street.

The sex was fun enough, but it wasn't about having fun; it was about taking some control. After that night, it would take another four months before I would have sex again. That was when I met my first boyfriend. Dutch showed up in May in my year of firsts.

He was a tall, princely Sri Lanken who was the perfect first boyfriend. We met at the gym; our first date was burgers and a beer at a pub near Thirtieth Street Station.

He was charming, a good kisser, and had a thousand stories about all the countries he had visited. And, he liked to keep busy. We had dinner with friends, took weekend trips to New York and the Jersey Shore. There was constant movement in Dutch's life; it was exactly what I needed. All this activity kept me distracted, and for a while I believed it was what I wanted.

But by the end of the summer, it was clear to me we weren't a good match. Distraction was turning to dissatisfaction. I moved into that first autumn bored in my relationship, haunted in my town, disinterested in my work, disillusioned with my family. And still no exit strategy. During a trip to Boston with Dutch that fall, I met a friend of his who was studying acupuncture and completing some of her practicum hours at a clinic in town called AIDS Care Project. I kept asking her questions, fascinated with the stories she shared about how this clinic was helping people with AIDS in ways Western medicine couldn't.

When she said she worked with a number of patients diagnosed with neuropathy and was helping them feel better, I was sold. I returned from the trip already decided I would be working at AIDS Care Project. I needed to get my acupuncture license, which meant moving to Boston, and just like that, I had my exit plan.

I returned to Boston one month later to look for an apartment, and I found a posting at a gym: two guys looking for a roommate. I gave them a thousand dollars to secure my place, and drove back to Philly wondering how I was going to make this work. My plan was pretty simple: find a waiter position and apply to acupuncture school. Any other details I'd take care as they showed up. It seemed like a good plan.

Suddenly, my year of firsts was filled with an unexpected series of lasts. Last meals with friends, last rent check, last walk through town, last day at work. For the last time, I stood on Arch Street, looking up at the apartment where Stephan and I danced with death a year earlier. At the end of my last meal with my parents, Mom, who didn't cry when I left home for college, broke down in tears as I hugged her goodbye.

And in this year of firsts, I swallowed my pride and, for the first time ever, asked my parents to borrow some money. Dad gave me a check for $1,000 when he hugged me, saying, "God Bless."

I piled the stuff I thought I'd need into a big U-Haul and left the rest on the side of the street. Little did I know I was driving right into what would be known as the Blizzard of '94, with Dutch in the passenger seat nervously playing copilot. I think of that drive as the labor pains in my rebirth. More than once, I thought we might die as I tried to control what felt like a tank, steadily heading up I-95. It was impossible to see, the roads were slick, and I had no real sense of the size of the U-Haul Truck I was driving.

But I was not stopping. I was on a mission! We arrived at my new apartment with fried nerves and every muscle in our bodies gripped tight. Somehow, through the deepening snow, Dutch and I managed to pull the bed out of the U-Haul and crashed on the floor of my empty bedroom with an empty pizza box and several beer bottles on the floor around us. We just wanted the day to be over.

But my first morning in my new city was very different. I sipped coffee and looked out the window at two feet of snow. No footprints (not even ours from last night), no piles and paths yet, just that pure whiteness across everything. The sun was bright, the air crisp and clean. It was like a huge greeting card made just for me. I didn't have a job, didn't really know anyone, and hadn't even applied to acupuncture school yet. And none of it mattered, because I knew. I knew, like I knew my name that I would become an acupuncturist and work at AIDS Care Project.

It would take four years, and a lot of hard work, but I was right. I marked the first anniversary of Stephan's death two weeks after moving to Boston. Sitting in my bedroom, I lit a candle and played his favorite music, cried a little, missed him a lot. I couldn't believe everything that happened in such a short time, and all of it without him. I felt guilty, and at the same time, I couldn't wait for whatever would happen in the coming months and years. I went to bed that night and checked my first year off the list.

I'd survived my year of firsts and was ready for whatever came next!

ACKNOWLEDGEMENTS

Getting this book edited, formatted and published was a labor of love, and wouldn't have happened without the support of some amazing, talented people I am fortunate to call my friends. My humble thanks to: Fern, Kelly, Lucy, John, Michelle, Rachel, Janet, Carin, and Bruiser for believing in me, and this book. Words cannot express how grateful I am for your contributions and support.

Timeline Bibliography:

The Kaiser Family Foundation

The Global HIV/AIDS Timeline/www.kff.org/
 (accessed July, 2010).

AIDS Aducation Global Information System, A Brief History of AIDS

www.aegis.com (accessed July, 2010).

www.wikipedia.org (accessed July, 2010).

About.com – The History of HIV: An HIV Timeline, by Mark Cichocki, R.N. (accessed, July, 2010).

Made in the USA
Middletown, DE
11 June 2020